Our Cause
for
His Glory

Our Cause *for* His Glory

Christianisation and Emancipation
in Jamaica

Shirley C. Gordon

The Press University of the West Indies
●Barbados ●Jamaica ●Trinidad and Tobago

The Press   University of the West Indies
1A Aqueduct Flats   Mona
Kingston 7   Jamaica

© 1998 by Shirley Gordon
All rights reserved. Published 1998

ISBN 976-640-051-2

02   01   00   99   98   5   4   3   2   1

Printed in Canada

CATALOGUING IN PUBLICATION DATA

Gordon, Shirley
   Our cause for his glory: christianisation and emancipation in Jamaica / Shirley Gordon
   p. cm.
   Includes bibliographical references and index.
   ISBN 976-640-051-2
   1. Missionaries – Jamaica – History.
   2. Church and education – Jamaica.
   3. Jamaica – Religion – African influences.
   I. Title.
   BV2848.J2G67 1998   291.7 dc-20

Cover illustration: *Madonna of Stony Gut*, Bas-relief carving.
Reproduced courtesy of the artist, Osmond Watson.

Book design by ProDesign Publishing Services,
Red Gal Ring, Kingston, Jamaica.

For my godchildren

Contents

Preface		*viii*
Acknowledgements		*xii*
Introduction		*xiii*
Abbreviations		*xviii*
Chapter 1	Postemancipation Perspectives	1
Chapter 2	European Missionary Christianity	10
	The Missionary Heyday	10
	Religious Education	13
	Promotion of Free Villages	26
	Decline of Missionary Christianity	29
Chapter 3	Jamaican Initiatives in Missionary Christianity	45
Chapter 4	Jamaican Christian Groups	69
Chapter 5	The Great Revival	86
Chapter 6	Social Consciences	96
Conclusion		120
Notes		127
Bibliography		137
Index		144

Preface

This is a second study concerning the Christianisation of Jamaica. The focus of both studies is the response of the Jamaican population to their varied encounter with the Christian religion. The first dealt with the impact of a missionary effort during slavery.[1] Three Moravian brothers arrived from Europe in 1754; the first black preachers from the southern states of America appeared from 1783 onwards. These were the pioneering Christian preachers from overseas. Emphatically, however, most Jamaicans first encountered Christianity through a much larger number of native leaders, deacons, elders, aids, variously named, and appointed by all missionary groups as a method of spreading the word as widely as possible. This was the practical method of proselytisation of all groups, both European missionary led and black American preacher led. The practice gave scope for Jamaican Christian initiatives in crowded city chapels and in scattered estate prayer groups alike. Their "hearers" were slave and free, and leaders and led interpreted the religious message in Jamaican forms of communication from the beginning.

Where slaves heard the teaching they were attracted to a religion which recognised their humanity, made many transfer their "ownership" to God rather than to their earthly masters, and reinforced their African belief in life after death. For free coloureds and blacks, who increased steadily in numbers as emancipation approached, the dissenting missions provided an arena for self-expression and the exercise of responsibility which they did not achieve in political life until 1831. In the scattered native Baptist groups originated by the American black Baptist preachers, particularly in the western parishes, a comparable initiative was organised in communication sustained by travelling preachers and their local leaders or "daddies". Their objective was the attainment of freedom for slaves; a definitive stage was reached in the "Baptist War" of 1831 to 1832.[2]

The growth of Jamaican Christianity took place in the long years between the birth of the anti-slavery movement in Britain and the final emancipation of slaves; American anti-slavery arguments, particularly in the black chapels, were also under discussion. Slaves and black freemen in Jamaica undoubtedly heard of both movements and increasingly anticipated their own freedom. In the thirty years between the abolition of the British slave trade and the final emancipation of British slaves, many of them sustained a vision of their prospective status in a free society. The mission chapels in particular provided them with a model of self-assuring "respectability" and modest living standards when the time came. Slaves saved money from market sales and hired out services, bought the freedom of their children where they could and, in the last decade of slavery, sought with determination the literacy which might prepare them for a better life. The ex-slaves were by no means unprepared for freedom as the British Government and most European missionaries feared. The question was rather whose interpretation of freedom would prevail.

The first thirty years of the free society covered by this second study witnessed many new Jamaican initiatives, related strongly to the actual experiences of life in the new civil state. In the process the people adopted, adapted and to a large extent themselves promoted their chosen forms of the Christian religion. A growing population of freed people, and their children who had not experienced slavery, developed a far greater variety of ideas and aspirations than their slave forebears. Furthermore, the experience of different families became ever more diverse as their individual fortunes varied; it could range from successful upward social mobility for a minority, who struck lucky with a crop or a small business, to distressing poverty for the many, unable to find either employment or land in the declining economy after the mid 1840s. Christian allegiance became correspondingly diversified, ranging from solid but declining membership of the Protestant missionary chapels, to a variety of uncoordinated religious groups synthesising native Baptist observances with Afro-Jamaican religious survivals. The missionaries were largely supported by "the respectable classes". The native groups attracted the increasing numbers who were reduced to a subsistence lifestyle.

This study attempts to explain a complex religious community divided broadly between a Euro-Christian tradition derived from the mission chapels, with islandwide denominational as well as metropolitan organisation, and an increasingly popular uncoordinated locally developed Afro-Christian tradition. The latter drew on the activities and the language of the chapels mingled with African derived religious expression, more particularly spontaneous participation of worshippers, communion with the spirit world of the ancestors and of nature and the charismatic leadership of their own people. To a considerable extent it was the divide between the literate who could use for themselves the inspiration of the Bible and the illiterate who preferred a spirit inspired religion.

Not only was Christianity divergent and individually interpreted, but the Afro-Christian version was anathema to the European missionary commentators who virtually ignored the parallel growth of local Jamaican Christianity until the Great Revival of 1861 demonstrated its undoubted strength all over the island. The ambivalent attitudes of the missionaries who reported the happenings revealed their ignorance as much as their ultimate disapproval of the turn of events associated with the revival. Similarly four years later the majority of European missionaries condemned the native Baptists for what they regarded, and much feared, as a race revolt against the white population in 1865.

Since ministerial writing provides the main source for the history of Christianity in the decades following emancipation, the historian faces a formidable task of interpretation. It is a fair inference that at least half the population had adopted some form of Afro-Christian religion by the 1860s. Since their communication was essentially immediate, localised and nonliterary they made a minimal lasting record for the historian. We are therefore confined to quotations of their point of view, usually expressed when protesting about a particular issue or otherwise vigorously demonstrating their feelings about a perceived injustice or, in the case of revival activities, an assertion of their own identity and religious preferences. The thoughts and attitudes of at least half of the contemporary Jamaican population have to be interpreted through their actions and occasional representations to the authorities rather than through the direct communication of, for example, a sustained missionary or governmental correspondence with headquarters in Britain. The fact that the native led Christian groups developed strong community loyalties in the face of economic hardship and little recognition in courts of local justice demonstrates that religion, conducted with apparent abandon on the Lord's Day, at other times soberly guided mutual help and the articulation of socioeconomic need. The petitions of the mid 1860s for access to land and for fair dealings in the planter dominated magistrates' courts were the product of the newly literate members of Jamaican village communities expressing the interests of their fellows as discussed in weekday gatherings in their meeting houses and other religious venues. The Afro-Christian concern for socioeconomic recognition in this world, related to their spiritual belief in the next, was surely articulated by the 1860s.

Finally, it is a suggestion of this study that Christianity in Jamaica was most native, and least derivative, at this stage of its history. In the Euro-Christian chapels the small native ministry was already producing its first articulate leaders who demonstrated, as well as claimed, a particular understanding of their own people and a particular concern for their development. In the diverse Afro-Christian tradition, not only were independent forms of charismatic worship established, but new socioeconomic aspirations were articulated in Bogle's call for "black awareness". In short the Jamaican roots in both Christian traditions were well planted. On the one hand the black awareness preached by Garvey and the Rastafarians in this century was heralded in the mid nineteenth by the native Baptists. Paul Bogle, for instance, regarded the solidarity of Jamaican black people as a religious principle to be asserted by children of God in their earthly society.[3] On the other hand the Jamaica Council of Churches, formed in 1941, is a logical development from arguments in favour of a Jamaican orientation to the Euro-Christian tradition, and has now produced advocates for "the decolonisation of theology".

Much of American pentecostalism which has arrived in Jamaica since the 1860s has neither engaged itself with matters of social concern nor with the strengthening of independent Jamaican identity. If this is a fair judgement of much modern Christianity it can be said that the Jamaican initiatives of the postemancipation years represent a more independent base for authentic Christian expression now. The challenge appears to be, not only to decolonise theology, but also to reconcile at last the Afro-Christian tradition with the Euro-Christian in Jamaican religious life. The historian can only discuss the origins of the double Christian inspiration.

Acknowledgements

The records of missionary societies in Britain are overwhelmingly the source material for this study. The letters and reports of their missionaries in the field offer a fund of island wide information on their activities and opinions. From this rich source one can extract a fair account of the response to their mission to convert the postemancipation population of Jamaica.

In addition the despatches of a highly prejudiced US Consul in Kingston add an extra dimension to the account. I am most grateful for the missionary societies concerned for the further use of their archives, without which no book would be possible on this theme. I am indebted to the Librarian and staff of the Angus Library at Regent's Park College, Oxford for access to the West Indian papers of the Baptist Missionary Society; to the Archivist and library staff of the School of African and Oriental Studies, University of London, for the extensive use of the microfiche copies of the archives of the Wesleyan Methodist and London Missionary Societies in their care; to the Librarian at Moravian Church House for access to her manuscript papers there, and to the Church Missionary Society in London for facilitating access to their records.

In Jamaica, I again thank Kathleen Miles for her matchless skill in transforming a rough typed manuscript sent from London into a completed version for the publisher. Lastly I am most grateful to Osmond Watson for permission to use *Madonna of Stony Gut* on the cover of a book so much in empathy with his carving.

Introduction

Christian teaching had already made a considerable impact on the population of Jamaica by 1838 when the slaves were finally emancipated. European missionaries had been arriving for the past eighty years, steadily increasing in number in the thirty years between the abolition of the slave trade and the end of slavery. Black preachers from the United States had travelled through the island for over half a century. The missionary preachers, white and black, appointed their Jamaican converts as leaders to expand Christian teaching far beyond the reach of limited numbers of overseas missionaries. The Christian message had thus been encountered through a variety of agents in the towns and on the estates. The black and coloured population, slave and free, were overwhelmingly the followers and aspiring members of the chapels and prayer groups which had arisen throughout the island. The white population, which had formerly been least in contact with missionary Christianity, were reached more systematically by the Established Church after Jamaica became an Anglican see in 1825.

Preaching was the first form of Christian communication, vigorously delivered alike by European dissenting missionaries and American black Baptist preachers. Large gatherings attended chapel services, preaching stations and impromptu groups on the estates as opportunity offered. Hearing the Word was not a commitment to Christianity, indeed the vast majority of hearers did not seek membership; it was however a means of learning the main tenets of the religion and of acquiring much of the language, the rhetoric and indeed the style of Christian utterance.

By 1838 deacons, leaders, aids, elders, in the terminology of different missions, greatly outnumbered missionaries and preachers from overseas.

Introduction

The majority of Jamaicans must have learnt their first Christian principles, if not extensive doctrine, from their fellow countrymen and women. The leaders prepared most candidates for baptism and subsequently supervised members to maintain missionary moral standards and chapel discipline.

Active participation in Christian practices ranged from responsible leadership in the mission chapels, on the one hand, to independent prayer meetings of native Baptists in slave quarters, on the other. It was also expressed in the adoption of Christian symbols, terminology and hymns in the Afro-Jamaican activities of Myal, the synthesis in Jamaica of the religious traditions of the various African communities from which the slaves had been taken. Myal groups infiltrated the native Baptists and/or maintained their own observances, claiming the authority of Jesus Christ for their activities. Individual choice seems to have been largely determined by encounter and opportunity. Even when choice was available, syncretism of Christian and African practices remained very common. Furthermore, people at any one time supported both, or moved from one to the other, according to perceived need. European missionaries were disconcerted by the love of emotional participation and the audible response to their own emotive preaching, not to mention energetic funeral activities by those attending Christian burials.

The Christian message, for the slaves who had encountered it from the earliest European missionaries, offered a spiritual freedom which helped them to transcend their earthly bondage. They could relate the Christian heaven in life after death with their own long held desire for the return of the departed spirit to Africa. Baptism and Christian burial had affinities with African religious practices and offered a special identity to slaves who adopted them, and expressed great happiness in so doing. There were numerous examples of Christian piety and tenacious faith among slaves with no other prospects of personal satisfaction in their lives. The spirituality which could rejoice in belonging to God rather than to the earthly master was perhaps most evident before prospects of worldly freedom became at least a distant possibility. The Christian belief that all men and women are equal before God was compelling whether the consequences were deferred to the afterlife or could be looked for in the world on earth. Slave interpretation of the doctrine became increasingly optimistic as a temporal aspiration during the long years in which their eventual freedom became ever more likely.

Introduction

The opportunities for communication, organisation and status in chapels and religious groups offered scope for members to act on their own behalf in matters beyond spiritual expression. First the free coloured population saw their chance for self-expression and the exercise of responsibility as stewards and leaders in the European dissenting chapels. Deprived until 1831 of political participation, they developed considerable influence in the religious sphere. In so doing they further provided models for later generations of manumitted and freed slaves ever increasing in number until the total emancipation of 1838. The respectability and responsibility engendered by the dissenting missions offered an arena in the search for recognition and status for many generations of free blacks and coloureds in a colony dominated by a minority white population in both economic and political concerns.

The black Baptists increasingly provided an equivalent solidarity to their own membership by offering regular meeting places and their own preachers. Outside Kingston their groups were largely estate centred with contacts maintained by travelling preachers. Native preachers and leaders were open in their espousal of the ultimate goal of freedom for slaves. European missionaries by contrast were forbidden by their home societies to express views on slavery in the slave colonies.

As emancipation became increasingly a real prospect, the Christian religion offered an imperative for freedom to its Jamaican followers. The planters and assemblymen who opposed missionary activity saw it as a revolutionary doctrine which would stir the slaves to seek freedom and equal civil status. Their fears were increased both by the example of the Haitian slave rebellion and by the anti-slavery campaign in Britain. The white establishment had reason to believe that Christian teaching and the development of Christian organisations could offer both the justification for and the channels of communication by which the slaves might in the long run promote their own freedom. In the last three decades of slavery in particular the Christian religion developed a temporal significance for the slaves who adopted it well beyond the promise of freedom and bliss in the world to come which had given solace to the earliest slave converts.

In postemancipation society the future development of Christianity in Jamaica had several prospects. The varying fortunes of the different agencies are the subject of this book. With hindsight most of the trends and outcomes were predictable once "persistent poverty" became obviously the condition of the majority of the ex-slave population and their offspring. The respectability and other worldly piety sought by European missionaries for ex-slaves is one strand in the story, more apparent in the first than the second respect. Another development was the assertion of Jamaican initiatives both in the Euro-Christian chapels and in the Afro-Christian communities. In different modes they sought to meet the problems of the times with the social values of the Christian religion as they variously perceived them. The followers of the European mission chapels increasingly added to their respectability and aspirations for status a nonconformist Protestant voice seeking fair prospects in their own society as they experienced the limitations of a colonial regime, in both its political and commercial aspects. For the native Christian groups solidarity and the protection of their own mutual interests were their response to the various hardships of the times.

In a free society there was opportunity for much more variety of expression and action than by definition there could have been under slavery. The story of the people's initiatives in seeking their own ambitions in freedom is therefore more complex than in the period where these ambitions had little scope for realisation. The purpose of this study is to describe the role of Christianity in all its manifestations, in contributing towards Jamaican initiatives in the first three decades of postemancipation society.

The documentation remains overwhelmingly the letters, resolutions and petitions of the missionaries of the European societies. There are, however, many more Jamaican written sources than had been the case in slavery. A small but determined group of Jamaicans themselves became missionaries to their own people; they wrote to the "home" societies in the same way as their European colleagues, but often in very different vein. Memoranda and petitions increased in number as issues arose in a variety of chapel communities. The town stewards, leaders and members made a practice of stating their views directly to the societies in London, sometimes against the missionaries on the ground, sometimes in support of them. In the postemancipation years, with the spread of literacy, expressions of opinion emerged in writing from a much wider variety of communities. Even where the majority of petitioners were illiterate it is clear that they had come to understand this form of communication and were convinced of its effectiveness in drawing attention to their various causes. There was an optimistic belief in the power of the written word which had emerged from the experiences of participation in the chapels

Introduction

and religious groups and from communication skills learnt in the elementary schools of the missions. Not only the language but also the attitudes adopted derived from a Jamaican understanding of the social context of the Christian religion. The mission schools taught their pupils to read the Bible, prayer books and hymn books; the language of literacy was therefore heavily biblical. On the other hand the skill of literacy opened up a wider literature wherever it could be obtained. The newspapers became accessible and provided another important source for the historian of the period, as they must have done for a slowly growing literate public. In short, Jamaican opinions of all sorts became increasingly available.

The missionaries of the postemancipation years frequently grieved because they now found their members less spiritual and less devout than the converts during slavery. Since the missionary purpose was largely concerned with creating an orderly hard-working labour force among ex-slaves, they should not have been surprised that their members had their own secular interests in adopting Christianity. It is the thesis of this study that the Christianisation of Jamaica in fact developed as a series of responses to, on the one hand, the apparent socioeconomic advantages offered in a free society or conversely, on the other, to the limitations of the free state revealed in the distressing actualities of the postemancipation decades. The duality of the development between European Christian observances and the practices of the Afro-Christian groups seemed to reflect the varied experiences of different sections of the population. In neither case was it a religion to escape the trials of this world; it was rather one to support people in finding their own lifestyles in a poor country which offered ex-slave generations little other scope for self-expression in their efforts to establish an acceptable identity in freedom.

Abbreviations

BMS	Baptist Missionary Society
CMS	Church Missionary Society
CO	Colonial Office
JBU	Jamaica Baptist Union
JRC	Jamaica Royal Commission, 1866
LMS	London Missionary Society
MMS	Moravian Missionary Society
SPG	Society for the Propagation of the Gospel
WMMS	Wesleyan Methodist Missionary Society

CHAPTER 1

Postemancipation Perspectives

Remember that he only is free whom the truth makes free.
Manifesto for Underhill meetings, attributed to
George William Gordon, August 1865

The religious life of the Jamaican people in the three decades following full emancipation of the slaves was largely influenced by their socioeconomic prospects in the new free society and by their changing fortunes in the declining prosperity of the island. Emphatically, however, they adopted Christian religious expression in a variety of forms in their encounters with the hard experiences of the times. In the first euphoria of freedom the European Protestant missions seemed to provide the greatest support for the aspirations of ex-slaves who had been preparing for a modest life of self-sufficiency for many years before they were free to pursue it. Thirty years later "native" churches in great variety had become the major form of Christian membership; they provided community support and activities which their members needed in the struggle to make a livelihood after the sugar industry had declined and many natural disasters had checked the market prospects for small farmers. The experiences of these years caused a marked difference between the minority who over the generations managed to remain upwardly mobile and achieve new social status, and those who became progressively poorer enduring constant hardship as the years went by.

The varying fortunes of ex-slaves and their children were reflected in their religious life. The moderately successful added to their growing status by accepting the European Protestant standards of respectability and moral rectitude in the missionary chapels. Those who looked for the means of dealing with the evils that they found in their situation developed native forms of Christian observance drawing on their Afro-Jamaican preferences in worship and in forms of personal participation very different from those sanctioned in the mission chapels. Jamaican Christianity was divided between a European Protestant model and a great variety of Afro-Jamaican versions. People supported one or both, changed their allegiance according to opportunity or preference and increasingly regarded the syntheses and changes as their own. One of the most emphatic benefits of freedom was exercised in a variety of activity in religious life which largely escaped the control of the colonial authorities. Pentecostal, spontaneous and participatory activities prevailed among the native Baptists, the independent Methodists and, as "Minister" Beckwith put it to the Royal Commission enquiring into the disturbances in 1865, any group such as his own "who simply desire to be called Christians".[1] Denominationalism was not the first concern of most Jamaican Christians in the years following emancipation. They probably developed their own versions more systematically in these decades than at any later time.

The missionary heyday was undoubtedly in the first years following full emancipation. For the mass of the ex-slaves it was the beginning of an ongoing struggle to find their identity and lifestyle in a community where they were now legally full British citizens. The missionaries, who during slavery had been under orders from their home societies to refrain from any comment on the evils of the system, were now charged with the duty of preparing their members to become a willing, obedient, hard-working labour force to maintain the declining sugar industry. The British Government for a period subsidised the religious educational efforts for the purpose, and planter opposition was somewhat stilled by an apparent new community of interest. The free workers themselves found support for their own aspirations for freedom in social status to be gained from chapel allegiance, if not full membership. Benefits included were the opportunity to become literate in the mission Sunday schools, missionary assistance in purchasing parcels of land and creating settlements of the newly free, and the day school education which helped the minority who could afford it to leave the land and find new status as teacher/catechists, clerks, policemen, storekeepers, and even bookkeepers.

Where these were real prospects the missionaries could pursue their role as architects of a respectable, God-fearing, sober living new generation of free Jamaicans, albeit hardly promoters of the declining sugar industry.

Any hope that the dissenting missions would be the final vehicle for the conversion of Jamaica to Christianity must have died by the mid 1840s when the British Government grant for religious education of ex-slaves was withdrawn and when the preferential treatment for colonial sugar was ended by the British Sugar Duties Act of 1846.[2] This act led to further closing of sugar estates in Jamaica with lack of employment and low wages randomly paid. The introduction of indentured labour further reduced the employment and remuneration of Jamaican workers. Thus began the long years where the majority were reduced to subsistence living and young people became increasingly mobile in search of work and the mutual support of communal living. Native versions of Christianity thrived in adversity. They were localised and accessible as the missionaries became less visible in scattered and distant settlements; their leaders were of the community, often former leaders of the mission chapels; they dealt with immediate problems in terms which people understood; they used Afro-Jamaican forms of worship and encouraged practices which illiterate people could participate with conviction. Dreams, visions, the getting of the spirit were experiences in the community setting which offered personal identity and support for people increasingly marginalised by circumstances from any other progressive elements in the island.

The epidemics which swept through Jamaica in the early 1850s caused the last wave of recruitment to the missionary congregations.[3] Most missionaries saw the afflictions as a visitation of divine wrath to encourage a godless people to turn to the Christian Lord. The afflicted people came to the chapels, welcomed the pastors in their homes as visitors to the sick and dying and recruited their services in the mounting number of funerals. In many cases missionaries and their families provided the only European medical services and drugs available to residents in parishes with only one colonial medical officer. When the years of epidemics were followed by seasons of drought, hurricane or flood which damaged the food crops, the missionary resource was not so attractive to the majority. Dues for classes, fees for day schools and collections at services could not be found. For many households it became impossible to provide the Sunday clothes which chapel attenders both wanted, and were expected, to wear. The missionaries themselves, urged to self-sufficiency by their home societies, were increasingly dependent on chapel dues, and to a considerable extent shared the poverty of their members. Financial considerations to maintain the missions at all became the major concern of missionary correspondence; the final conversion of Jamaica was no longer a feasible objective for foreign missions and was seldom mentioned by them after the mid 1840s.

The conversion which had always been substantially the achievement of the Jamaican leaders, deacons, and catechists of the European missions continued in the same hands, but increasingly independent of the missions. Native Jamaican Christian groups usually called themselves Baptist, and were referred to as "Native Baptists" by those who recorded their existence. There were also independent Methodists; others followed a variety of individual Christian preachers who had gained acceptance in their communities. They had no islandwide organisation, no written records and only local contact with each other. The travelling black preachers during slavery were largely replaced by resident black pastors, particularly in the new settlements of freeholders arising in the postemancipation years. There were two substantial native Baptist chapels in Kingston surviving from the long pastorate of the American George Liele and his followers in the city.[4] Similarly the groups fostered by Moses Baker in the western parishes had a continuous existence.[5] The native Baptists were also a force in the parishes of St Catherine, Clarendon and St Thomas-in-the-East, where black itinerant preachers on the estates had long visited the people in areas not reached by the European missionaries. Not only were black Baptist groups well established in their own strongholds, they were aggressive against encroachment by Europeans into the districts where black preachers were already established. They increasingly argued that Jamaican people were best served in their Christianity by black natives like themselves who were committed to the country and who would not leave their flocks to return to an overseas home.

Immediately following emancipation the native Baptists were limited in their recruitment in that they did not yet offer schooling for ambitious ex-slaves. Their preachers were often illiterate themselves. The early popularity of the missions at the time was largely, if not overwhelmingly, due to their provision of Sabbath and day schools, in that order of magnitude, where children and adults could learn to read. Literacy was the early aspiration of thousands of ex-slaves; if they could afford to send their children to the church day schools the next generation could add to their educational attainments writing, computation and a formidable quantity of British focused general knowledge, learnt by rote. Elementary schooling provided the opportunities for social mobility, usually departure from agricultural work, for the first generations of the successful postemancipation families. Although many teacher/catechists emerged from the day schools to ensure the survival of the European missions, the missionaries soon noted with great disappointment that their ex-day school pupils did not to any great extent become members of their denominational congregations. Undoubtedly many were, or became, native Baptists and used their elementary education to promote their own concerns.

Another strong recruitment to the native churches came from leaders of the mission chapels who broke away with their groups to form local associations independent of European authority. Invariably they ignored those British nonconformist moral standards ardently sought by the missions which were at variance with Jamaican norms. The defection from the mission chapels, or the practice of supporting both mission services and native Christian meetings, meant an increase in literate members in the native Baptist groups with some experience of the "missionary culture". Many independent Jamaican preachers wore the black gowns used by European pastors and included the Lord's Supper in their range of religious services. Native Baptist chapels and meeting houses were built in many settlements and became the centre for community debate and decision making; the most notable example was the then recently built chapel at Stony Gut where Paul Bogle assembled with his followers in 1865.[6] Native preachers and deacons were established and supported by local communities as a progression from the itinerant preachers and illiterate leaders of the past.

A significant component of the black Baptist population was American. Black American Baptists can be identified in Jamaica from missionary records consistently until emancipation. They seem to have been particularly influential in the western parishes where missionaries reported them as "highly intelligent, but . . . very contemptuous of white ministers".[7] In the years between the British and the American emancipation of slaves, Robert Harrison, the American Consul stationed in Kingston, encountered much difficulty from a steady flow of black Americans, slave and free, finding their way into Jamaica. A fanatically pro-slavery man himself he constantly deplored the advent of what he termed "native American missionaries of the Anti-Slavery Society".[8] Very few Americans are mentioned in the records of the British missionary societies; only the LMS received some half a dozen American Congregationalists, almost certainly all white. The consul's fulminations suggest many more. If so they must have been independent preachers who no doubt worked with Jamaican independent groups.

Much more frequently the consul was bothered by the concerns of large numbers of black American sailors, again slave and free, who deserted from their ships and were granted their freedom by local magistrates in Jamaica. The consul described this as "a situation in which I am frequently placed".[9] There is little indication of the religious allegiance of these new arrivals into the colony, but much evidence of the considerable popular support for their liberation in Jamaica. In typical condemnation the consul wrote, "Any Negro who now wishes to desert an American vessel has only to pick up the most depraved of his colour in the streets to swear that he knows said Negro to be a slave and he will be released from his engagement at once."[10]

The significance of the consul's information is not only that black Americans sought refuge in Jamaica before the general emancipation of slaves in the United States, but also that their liberation in the colony was a popular cause. This phenomenon is not mentioned by the British missionaries, which suggests that the active supporters of black American seamen seeking their freedom were native Baptists and other independents in the Jamaican ports. The cause was both an anti-slavery issue, but also prompted by black solidarity. "Such is the power and audacity of the Negro population here just now, heightened by a plentiful distribution of *Uncle Tom's Cabin*," complained the American Consul, "that they would take any of their colour out of an American Vessel, be they free or otherwise."[11] Despite the consul's marked prejudice his reports reveal that Jamaican black and coloured people could take up the cause of fellow blacks from abroad and deplore the continuation of American slavery as their own concern, despite their own vicissitudes.

Beginning in the last quarter of 1860 a Great Revival swept across the island, lasting for several months into mid 1861. It was led strongly by young people who had not experienced slavery, but who were now the most destitute victims of the prevailing poverty of the times. Despite their own early optimism over the Revival, the missionary pastors were unable to contain the spontaneous religious movement of the people. The Great Revival has been regarded as a triumph of the African survival of Myal religion.[12] What seems more likely is that it was a triumph of the native Christian groups who had accommodated Myal practice as the European groups had never learnt to do. The Great Revival was a Jamaican popular initiative demonstrating the values which had been adopted, and adapted, from the Jamaican Christian experience as perceived by the younger population at a time of mounting hardship. It was an acceptance of the missionary insistence of the importance of repentance for sin, albeit in a demonstrative fashion which the pastors could not control, associated with many propitiatory activities to contend more immediately with the evils of the day. Traditional Myal practices could be applied to current suffering more apparently than the services of a Christian denomination, which in any case took time and money to join. The obvious resource was to support both, with a preference for the native groups when rampant misfortune seemed more of a problem than European protestant concepts of sin and repentance. The missionaries were beginning to realise that they were not opposing heathenism, as they had so long asserted, but what they now considered to be a dilution of Christianity.

By the 1860s the economic plight of the island was exacerbated by the effects of the American Civil War on the North American trade. Prices of foodstuffs, clothing and household requirements soared at a time when cash was already a scarce commodity for the majority of the people. The House of Assembly did nothing to reduce the heavy taxation that they imposed on the population, and in the many years when natural disaster afflicted home production, destitution resulted. It was out of this situation that arose the momentous events of 1865 and the emergence of an articulate Jamaican leadership at both grassroots and a fledgling middle class level.

The challenge to European authority in the Christian churches grew not only among those who broke away from them, but also within their membership. Stewards, deacons, leaders and members of chapels claimed rights to decision making and disputed the ownership of buildings erected with their contributions of cash and labour. Teachers trained at the Mico Institution and at denominational training schools took over from European teachers in the day schools at an early stage after emancipation.[13] Jamaican teachers became the lay preachers who sustained the expanding stations which the missionaries could now only occasionally visit; gradually individual Jamaicans became assistant missionaries and then were ordained as full pastors. The whole question of the role of a native ministry emerged with particular reference to their relative standing and relationship with European missionary pastors. This was certainly a pending issue by the 1860s.

In the critical year of 1865 two petitions were addressed to the colonial authorities by small farmers.[14] "Resolutions following the Underhill meetings were written and presented by people from all over the island who had learnt sufficient literary skill to present their case for themselves. Whether in formal Victorian English or in simple direct statements, Jamaicans stated their own case for more land, for justice in the planter dominated magistrates' courts and for less oppressive taxation. They had adopted social attitudes deriving from the current British nonconformist conscience concerning social evils, on the one hand, grafted onto a native community spirit, on the other, which identified and tackled current local problems as an aspect of collective religious life. The emphasis in different districts appeared to follow the prevailing form of Christian allegiance in each.

The missionary culture remained with the minority who could sustain their upward social mobility in hard times; their adoption of European moral standards and lifestyles was the symbol of their success in the process. The varied responses to the Morant Bay disturbance and its sequel reflect the variety in the perceptions of the Christian religion in Jamaican society by 1865 was somewhat demonstrated by . The protest at the courthouse which became a riot on 11 October was led by a native Baptist deacon and his followers. The authorities variously interpreted this demonstration as a native Baptist rising most alarmingly in the island at large or at least in the parish of St Thomas-in-the-East. In the overreaction to the event the troops particularly targeted native Baptist preachers and their followers in the bloody aftermath of suppression.

Most European clergy and missionaries sympathised with the plight of the people as expressed in the Underhill Letter, although the majority were not participants in the parish meetings to discuss it. They were nevertheless very ready to accept the official view of the riot in St Thomas-in-the-East as the beginning of a well-planned islandwide rebellion to secure the land for black people. Only the savagery of the repression during martial law in the parish caused some, particularly the few Jamaican missionaries, to change their sympathies. Indeed several British missionaries were warned by their home societies against their ill-considered stance in condemning the Jamaican people at large and, in many cases, condoning the violent retribution. This interpretation of events was certainly not shared by the nonconformist congregations in British chapels who collected funds for their missions abroad.

The poles of Christian allegiance, and the variety of its expression in postemancipation Jamaica are the theme of this study. The religious impulse of the people was undoubtedly strong; it had to find expression in dire times for the majority of the population. The European missionary culture provided an acceptable model for those who could improve their circumstances in a colonial society promoting current British social values; they found their self-expression and identity in this setting. For those for whom a subsistence living seemed the only prospect Afro-Jamaican Christianity provided not only a spiritual support; it also offered forms of community loyalty which could be applied to the problems of poverty and their considerable marginalisation from the colonial society. The differences between Euro-Christianity and Afro-Jamaican Christianity were in social terms very wide. Both, however, offered scope for exceptional initiatives and strong convictions from their own leaders and their followers which was lacking in other aspects of colonial life. In the churches, chapels and native meeting houses Jamaicans found a focus for self-expression using communication skills learnt in the Sabbath and day schools, and a characteristic self-confidence learnt in the school of their own experience of postemancipation life. Their representations derived from Christian values as developed in different sections of the island community.

CHAPTER 2

European Missionary Christianity

*Minister, some of us dying for de Gospel;
but me can't say for other people.*
Quoted Seddon's Journal, 1838

The Missionary Heyday

The most effective European missionary period in Jamaica was undoubtedly during the apprenticeship before full emancipation and in the five years following. The BMS missionary, James Phillippo, writing in 1843 observed the rapid recent growth of the mission chapels and opined that the task of conversion was nearly completed.1 It is probable that some half of the population at that point were members of dissenting chapels or the expanding Established Church, or both.[2] The rest were certainly aware of missionary messages; they formed the body of "hearers" and "enquirers" who gathered in their hundreds to hear the Sunday preachers and, for a time, to attend the annual thanksgivings in the missionary chapels to thank the Lord, with the British Government and people, for the blessing of freedom.

There is no doubt that the popularity of the dissenting missions in the early days of freedom derived from a perceived concordance between missionary objectives and the social aspirations of the newly free to find an acceptable status in society. The "missionary culture" of respectability, personal recognition and responsibility, with improved living standards both moral and material, appealed as a model to aspiring ex-slaves.

Furthermore the pre-emancipation generations of free coloureds and blacks had found status and self-respect in the dissenting chapel communities. They now presented many examples of considerable upward social mobility, ranging from the first coloured members in the House of Assembly to the many poor, but independent, freeholders with parcels of land in remote parts of the island. The more recently emancipated found the same potential support in the missions and espoused the European Christian code accordingly.

The dissenting missionaries themselves had survived the active hostility of most of the plantocracy, the Colonial Church Union and systematic opposition from the House of Assembly.[3] They were no longer in danger of being expelled from the island as seditious sectarians. On the contrary they were now backed by the British Government to promote the development of an orderly, industrious and obedient labouring class in the ex-slave colonies. The missionaries for their part readily accepted the task not only of converting the population to the Christian faith, but as a corollary urging them to the acceptance of a labouring life as sugar workers in an acquiescent colonial peasantry. Missionaries who had over the years frequently cited their own rights as British citizens now undertook the project of inducting over 300,000 new British citizens in Jamaica into the social values and work ethic of Victorian, nonconformist, class conscious Britain.

Nevertheless, most missionaries deplored any exploitation and victimisation of their ex-slave members by former owners and overseers both during the apprenticeship and after 1838. Of the white population in Jamaica the missionary and his family were the most concerned for the rise of the newly free to respectable and modestly secure lifestyles. Where until the passing of the British Act of Emancipation the missionary policy in the field had been to keep silence on the evils of slavery, no such reticence was maintained over the evils of the apprenticeship. Most missionaries strongly condemned the exploitation of the apprentices in confusing their compulsory working hours with those qualifying for payment, the evictions from cottages and provision grounds on the estates, and the barbaric punishments meted out by the magistrates. They denounced the apprenticeship as demi-slavery and warned that if the praedial apprentices were not released at the same time as the nonpraedial in August 1838 there would be serious disorder, reminiscent of the Sam Sharpe rebellion in 1831.

In short the political sympathies of the missionaries in the decade after the Act of Emancipation were, on their own terms, for the emancipated people; it could hardly have been otherwise since the missions were now specifically committed to the moral and social progress of a newly freed labouring class. Many of the ex-slaves gladly accepted this championship and support for their own corresponding aspirations. The people were urged to work for fair wages and to pay for their own homes and services from the proceeds. They were also advised on what constituted a fair wage and fair working conditions. The BMS missionaries in particular cautioned their members in the first months of full freedom not to start working for the estates until these matters were resolved by their employers. For this the Baptists were dubbed by one Governor "the political parsons".[4] Missionary involvement in the working problems of their members at this initial phase of freedom must have been a great reassurance to ex-slaves, often bewildered by their change of circumstances and heading for sad disillusionment after the first euphoria of freedom. Chapel membership was an obvious support in finding stability while striving for upward mobility.

The emphatic phase of political activity among the BMS missionaries virtually lasted until the deaths of Knibb and Burchell in 1845 and 1846 respectively. These two in particular sought a political role for those ex-slaves who were early freeholders and so could at that point qualify to vote. Knibb's ambition was for black voters of the emancipated generation in due course to secure their own interest in the House of Assembly.[5] This he did not achieve, but the attempt in itself must have set new sights for the immediately more successful of the small freeholding population which expanded so rapidly in the first years of the 1840s.

The BMS interventions were directly to promote the standing of that section of the emancipated population who succeeded as small property owners making mostly modest, but regular, incomes by a combination of paid estate work and the proceeds from their food crops sold in the markets of the already growing towns and new settlements. The women of these families worked at home and their children were sent to the mission and church schools. The next generations became the future teacher/catechists and pursued other nonpraedial activities. The socially mobile in these terms were always the minority, but in the early years of freedom their example fed the aspirations of many others. Landholding, literacy and schooling seemed the essential prerequisites for such progress. The missions offered some of the best prospects for all three developments.

Religious Education

There is little doubt that in the years following the Emancipation Act missionary gains were at least as much due to their educational efforts as to their preaching. The ex-slaves had a driving desire for literacy, for their children and for themselves. It was a critically important aspect of their own perception of freedom. Throughout the apprenticeship Sunday classes for adults and children were an intrinsic part of Sabbath observance in virtually all chapels and many preaching stations. These were less successfully supplemented by evening classes, but most effectively by mutual instruction amongst the apprentices of all ages on the estates and at other work places throughout the week.

This was a case where the objectives of the missionaries and their followers for some time appeared to coincide. With initial support from the British Government in a Negro Education Grant the religious bodies were selected, and self-selected, as the agencies for the moral and religious instruction of the ex-slave population. For the missions schooling was now the priority activity in their conversion campaign. Religious instruction would attract the people to Christian church membership at the same time as it created a peaceful, hard-working agricultural labouring class. The socioeconomic purpose for religious education was the same as that simultaneously developed in elementary schooling for British working classes, namely the maintenance of an acquiescent labour force. The missionaries adopted equivalent objectives for popular education in post-slavery Jamaica with all the implications of stratified social class included. While the missionary purposes and those of the newly free were both mutually supportive and realistic in the state of the economy, religious education flourished. Day schools were opened in most stations; in the early years European teachers were brought out to teach in them and were partly paid from the British Government's Negro Education Grant. More popular still remained the Sabbath schools, held before and after the chapel services, where large classes of all ages were initiated into reading. They were taught by missionary wives and their families, by mainly coloured members who had been educated in private schools and increasingly by the newly literate themselves, again of all ages, teaching their fellows to read in the chapel classes as well as in their own homes and work places.

The church and chapel schools, day, Sabbath and evening, were attractive to their clients for different, but not entirely divergent, reasons. For the majority of those attending the purposes were specific; it was largely a matter of finding the opportunity to benefit from progressive stages of "religious education". Literacy was a goal for people of all ages; its pursuit for a period after emancipation amounted to a popular campaign wherever a Sabbath school could be reached. Elementary education at the day schools added writing, numeracy and a formidable quantity of Useful (European) Knowledge, learnt by rote, to the acquisition of those who could afford the time and the fees. These were progressively the qualifications for entry into occupations other than agricultural labour and domestic service, still essentially dominated by the conditions of slavery, and so abhorred by those who could escape them.

Most missionaries, notably Phillippo in Spanish Town, soon recognised the prospects for social mobility offered by their schools; they also depended on the day schools as nurseries for their own leaders in teaching and preaching to their own people. It was in fact not an agricultural working class that they were nurturing in the schools so much as an escape route to other occupations. Yet the British Government's purpose in encouraging religious education for a few years after emancipation was to create a peaceful peasantry ready to work on the sugar estates. The missionaries were intended to be both the agents and the articulate supporters of this aim. In the event an equation of Christianity with social order became a stronger missionary purpose for religious education than the maintenance of a labouring population for the declining sugar industry; this became their appeal as they begged funds and resources from British Christians to continue their work in religious education.

The heyday of missionary schooling was in the first five years of freedom while it seemed possible that this was the beginning of a system of popular education which would expand steadily as far as the need was expressed. The British Government's Negro Education Grant assisted religious bodies to build school houses and supplemented teachers' salaries. The full reality of the missions' commitment to education became alarmingly clear only when the British grant finally ended in 1845, after four years of gradual diminution. The Colonial Government could not be persuaded to accept any general responsibility for even a modicum of public education until the mid 1850s. The delay, and subsequently the limited popular support for schooling, made it certain that little could be available to the population at large. Elementary education was only to be the opportunity of those who could pay school fees to support a schoolmaster, who had enough funds to keep their children adequately dressed for school and who could spare their labour from the family income. The fact of the matter was that in 1846 the average attendance of children of 5-14 years at school was 12.6 percent of their number, and it had reached only 17 percent of the age group by 1864, out of a population which had expanded by nearly one-third between the first two censuses.[6] In short, elementary schooling had been achieved by less than one-fifth of the population by 1865. It was clearly the province of the minority who had attained their postemancipation socioeconomic aspirations to the extent of being able to pay for the commodity of an elementary education for their children. Increasingly too over the period the majority of families used their children's labour to maintain the family income; this was much encouraged by estate overseers as an excuse for paying even lower wages. Even with those who did, and do, attend the schools, the persisting poor attendance on Fridays before the Saturday markets, shows what a struggle it has remained to support children for daily elementary education.

The much easier accessibility of the Sabbath schools explains their persistence over the years. What was intended at first as a programme for literacy, with presumably a limited life, soon was recognised as the sole opportunity for instruction for the mass of the people. Sabbath schools remained on all stations during the 1850s and 1860s when many day schools were abandoned for lack of financial resources either to retain them or their teachers.

Missionary effort with the Sabbath schools was sustained with a growing realisation that this was their best remaining means of attracting more members. They increasingly discovered that people did not understand the sermons that they attended, and had little doctrinal knowledge. Reading seemed the only hope of getting them to abandon "their many foolish and superstitious notions" and in particular to cease their habit of going to the black preachers for information on what the white missionaries were trying to tell them. This practice particularly riled missionaries who persisted in their belief that all black preachers were themselves ignorant and illiterate. However, missionary descriptions of their Sabbath classes do not suggest that they achieved an increase in doctrinal understanding any better than that atttibuted to the black preacher

As the years went by attendees of Sabbath schools were not as impressionable: their teachers were correspondingly less ambitious. An LMS minister in Kingston, for example, had a class of 50-60 old women taught by an eight year old from the day school.[7] A new missionary to Grateful Hill was delighted to take over a Sabbath class of 200 "who gladden our hearts by their diligence and the avidity with which they commit to memory the Scriptures, Wesley's hymns and portions of the Conference Catechism";[8] one suspects that this was a Grateful Hill social occasion rather than an educational project. A third missionary report in the 1860s confirmed both the persistence of the Sabbath schools and the limited level at which they now operated; he reported a class of 230 at Mount Zion led by teachers who a few years back could not read themselves.[9]

It would appear that functional literacy was hardly the product of these later Sabbath schools. They offered instead religious instruction mainly by rote. The Jamaican ability to quote the Scriptures at length was no doubt born in the Sunday classes. It was here also that the less Euro-sophisticated chapel followers prepared themselves for membership. One expressing a preference for the Sabbath school over the sermon, explained that she never understood the sermon but could follow the Sunday school teachers.[10]

The evening class idea had been a promising one on the estates during the apprenticeship; it became less effective as people were progressively more dispersed in new settlements. It had most success where there was a collective population of adequate size for such activities. An example at Morant Bay showed the LMS missionary and his schoolmaster between them providing classes systematically four nights a week as follows:

Monday	Bible Class	(Missionary)
	Reading	(Schoolmaster)
Tuesday	Singing	(Missionary)
Wednesday	Writing	(Schoolmaster)
Thursday	Ciphering	(Schoolmaster)

After each class there was a Bible reading, "a few plain remarks", prayer and a hymn.[11] This does not appear to have been a grassroots programme for illiterates; rather it was an extended opportunity for those who had

European Missionary Christianity

learnt the elements of reading already. It was an urban initiative which had its successors.

In the day schools the missionary purpose failed not only for lack of resources to maintain them. Although the schools provided some chapel deacons, leaders and schoolmasters, the majority of their output did not even become members of the missions which had given them schooling. As religious education had been seen as the best method of advancing evangelisation this was a particular disappointment. Even the Moravians with their long-standing, relatively close-knit chapel communities in the central and western parishes bemoaned the fact that the youth educated in their schools had not joined their chapels. The majority, they acknowledged, had not been converted to their church nor even "touched by the grace of God". The Moravian missionaries, however, recognised "that the spread of education has added to their intelligence; that emancipation has given them liberty of thought as well as of action, and increased their independence of character".[12] The development of the last-mentioned quality seems particularly true. It can be assumed that for those who could afford to attend day schools their own aspirations for social mobility were reinforced, if only symbolically, by the fact of their elementary education. Furthermore they were in regular communication with each other walking, often long distances, to and from school. The postemancipation generations must have done much to develop new ideas and new aspirations amongst themselves.

The general response to missionary schooling may well be described by one of its products who in fact himself later became a schoolmaster and an assistant missionary. By his own account this future career was not the result of James Eastwood's schooling at Four Paths. "I early learned to read scripture", he later recalled, "but used to read it so heedlessly a manner [sic] that I understood (then) nothing of the truths contained therein, the fact is that I did not care to understand it; I read over the history of Christ's life and death as an idle tale or something which I thought did not concern me." Eastwood was in fact converted long after his schooldays; most of his fellows never were.[13] It is reasonable to assume that most of the day school pupils had more secular than religious concerns in attending; membership of the denomination which offered them schooling was certainly no assured sequel.

Since the day schools were supported by only a minority of the working people they had a tendency to cause new social divisions in their communities. The elementary school graduates were distanced from even their own families, not only because of their seemingly exclusive opportunities, but also by the nature of their instruction which increasingly resembled, in content as well as in method, that of British church elementary schools. The students' elders complained that they thought themselves superior and resented advice and guidance. This complaint emerged more strongly as the pupils were drawn from postemancipation generations which had no experience of slavery. They were clearly not inspired by parents and grandparents who reiterated accounts of the transformation they themselves had felt at their official emancipation. It was a likely outcome that internal and then external migration would develop as the aspiration of young people. Those with literacy and a certain fluency of communication would have the best prospects for employment away from home.

The education which made the young people think they were rising in the world, and which nourished their own spirit of independence, was in fact slated as wholly inappropriate by European observers in the mid century. The Moravian pastor, John Buchner, recognised as well as most both the aspirations and the setbacks of the postemancipation generations. He refuted suggestions that they were not intelligent, and certainly recognised their shrewdness in dealing with their own concerns. Elementary education did not, however, in Buchner's opinion meet the challenge of the times; it proved the remarkably sustained memory powers of its products; it did not prepare them for "thought and invention".[14] He could have added that these qualities were, nevertheless, largely developed in the vicissitudes of daily life. The future Colonial School Inspector, John Savage, invited by the Governor to report on elementary schooling in 1864, was even more thoroughgoing in his criticism. He found that the prevalence of rote learning of irrelevant "useful information" was "dabbling with mere words and dry, abstract figures". The elementary school "graduate" was left to enter working life "with scarcely a single practical principle or intelligent thought". Of the 490 schools in Jamaica in 1864 Savage rated only eight as first class in educational quality; seventeen as second class; one hundred and ten as third class, and one hundred and fifty-four as fourth class.[15] The remaining two hundred presumably did not rate at all. Despite this miserable educational record the day schools were not a failure for their clients. It was the fact that they had attended at all, rather than the standard

European Missionary Christianity

achieved which opened doors for the "graduates". Schooling, however inappropriate, remained a major opportunity for social mobility.

The religious bodies were defeated by their situation rather than complacent about the results of their schools. What in effect they did before the 1870s was to provide literacy and some symbols of knowledge to create opportunities for a decreasing minority of children from working class families. The majority of the population was untouched by their day school provision.

It was the need to provide Jamaican school teachers, missionaries and ultimately native pastors which caused the Moravians at Fairfield, the Presbyterians at Montego Bay, the Church Missionary Society at Grove and the Baptists at Calabar in Rio Bueno, to start training schools to take small numbers into further education. These enterprises did secure a better educated leadership for the missions. In preparing teacher/catechists they probably in fact saved the missionary purpose in their denominations. Without them the European pastors could never have maintained their stations, let alone expanded their activities after the early 1840s. Unlike the products of the elementary schools the handful of training school graduates were committed to the service of their mission denominations.

The training schools also provided the collegiate education of the few native pastors who did emerge in the middle of the century. The rate of their ordination was determined by each mission's degree of acceptance of the desirability of a native ministry. The BMS was early aware of the need for trained native ministers, and of an enlightened lay leadership, if their mission was to survive in Jamaica. Knibb, for instance, declared himself very ready to stand down as soon as Jamaicans could be prepared to service the Baptist Union Church in the island.[16] He was certainly a strong promoter of the opening of Calabar College at Rio Bueno in 1843. The first student was ordained from Calabar in 1847.[17] John Clarke in 1869 named nineteen other graduates of Calabar in a list of "native ministers" in that year.[18]

The early impetus for Calabar College was in fact to provide Jamaican ministers and missionaries for West Africa, hence its name. This was at the time also the main purpose of the home missionary society in assisting the opening of the college. The BMS Secretary, Angus, who visited the mission in Jamaica in 1846 to evaluate its current financial crisis, now also approved of the College specifically for the training of local ministers.

It would, he reported, provide additional pastors for the ever more dispersed preaching stations of the mission, and it would be cheaper to pay native rather than European missionaries. There were at this point eight students; those who had already left had become teachers and businessmen.[19]

The Presbyterian training school at Montego Bay also found that it trained more teachers than ministers. The Mico College continued to train candidates from most mission schools in modest numbers. It was the Mico graduates who largely replaced European teachers in the day schools as prejudices against coloured and black schoolmasters declined, or for want of any alternative, were suppressed.

The college and training school enrolments remained very small; financial limitations always prevented expansion or even maintenance of adequate tutorial services. In effect there was only a cumulative provision, from all sources, for at most fifty students in any post-elementary school training. This truncated educational opportunity was criticised by missionary and aspiring new citizen alike. A good example of the latter was the young schoolmaster Barrett McLean, who wrote directly and independently to the LMS begging them not to withdraw, but on the contrary to extend their educational programme. He had been a pupil at the LMS school at Brixton Hill, had been trained at Mico and then appointed to teach first at Four Paths and then back at Brixton Hill; he in addition preached alternately with the LMS missionary at the two stations every Sunday.

McLean asserted that most of the missionary work was in fact conducted by "forgotten and neglected native teachers" and yet they were paid a pittance. They were anxious to improve themselves, but could not afford books to do so. It was high time, maintained McLean, for the young men of Jamaica to have opportunities for their betterment. The LMS, for instance, up to this point had made no provision for training native ministers, although there were plenty of candidates available.[20] Barrett McLean was reproved by the LMS missionaries in Jamaica for taking this initiative; he was told that all letters to the LMS directors should in future be routed through his European missionary. He may not have been well pleased with this instruction since he had already expressed the opinion that the teacher/preachers were in fact carrying the brunt of the mission's work in his country. He was in any case undoubtedly expressing the frustration of many of his fellows who had outrun the education available to them and could see the great need for further opportunities to better themselves, not least to qualify for occupations currently occupied by Europeans.

Some of the schoolteacher/catechists had indeed acquired scholarly tastes and application on their own initiative. Atkinson, the Mico trained teacher at Ridgemount, had made himself proficient in Latin and had embarked on Greek and Euclid when his European pastor encountered him.[21] This was a considerable achievement in addition to running one of the largest elementary schools in Jamaica, preaching every Sunday and conducting evening classes during the week. The LMS missionaries' decision to open a training school at Ridgemount in 1856 may or may not have been influenced by McLean's representations and by the example of Atkinson and others. The declared purpose was to train native missionaries for Jamaica.

Had the LMS had the resources to maintain their college it might well have met the wider need for further education. Their three-year curriculum was planned and progressive and, in European terms, provided a balance between general further education and theological studies. It was developed as follows:

Year 1	Year 2	Year 3
English Grammar	Latin & Greek	Latin, Greek & Hebrew
Composition	Logic & Rhetoric	Mental & Moral Philosophy
Arithmetic	Mathematics	Biblical criticism
Geography	Natural Philosophy	Theology
History	Systematic Theology	Exposition, essays
Natural and Revealed Religion	Church History	Composition of sermons[22]
Latin	Essays & Composition of sermons	

The full-time students also conducted between them the teaching at the well-developed Ridgemount School. Part-time students, the married men, continued their duties as teacher/catechists at their home stations.

It says much for the quality, and the stamina, of the eight Ridgemount students that they faced their first examinations with considerable success, despite the preeminently European content of the curriculum. They satisfied missionary William Hillyer examining on Milligan, *Structure of the English Language* and Parts I & II of Milner's *Geography*. Missionary

James Milne examined the Latin, in which students read and construed portions of Caesar and Eutropius; James Eastwood, now a part-time student, was allowed to read Valpy's *Delectus*.23 The most interesting comments on the students' achievements came from Duncan Fletcher who examined them on Paley's *Natural Philosophy*. He reported that the candidates were well acquainted with the author's arguments; more significantly he found that some of them made "most ingenious remarks . . . evidently the result of their own observation". Furthermore Fletcher found that they gave "a pleasing indication of good reasoning powers and assiduous application".[24] The latter quality had been noted before in Jamaican students' ability to learn extensively by rote. The new element in Fletcher's comments was his recognition of their original reasoning powers. The short-lived Ridgemount experiment helped to dispel the notion that young Jamaicans emerging from their impoverished communities would not apply themselves to study or lacked good reasoning ability, even when applied to a very alien literature.

In the following year the students again did extremely well in their examinations, but only three remained in residence and only one was enrolled as a part-time student. The examiners remarked that the candidates were very promising as future classical scholars, but that their achievements were perhaps too ambitious for future assistant missionaries.[25] The 1858 Report on Ridgemount also regretted a lack of pious young men with the commitment to undertake the ministry. Since one student had withdrawn through lack of adequate finance to continue his studies and another with insufficient stamina to combine teaching and preaching with heavy studies of unfamiliar material, it seems inappropriate to have attributed lack of piety as the cause of poor recruitment to the training school.[26] In the event three of the five who completed the three-year course became assistant, not full, missionaries for the LMS mission. This limited outcome for all their efforts to achieve higher learning might in itself explain the lack of further candidates. Also the indications are that the aspiring young men were seeking secular at least as much as clerical advancement. It was a general further education that they sought rather than one that had limited chapel related prospects in view.

Isolated moves were made to meet the need for further education by the formation of Mutual Improvement Societies in one or two stations. William Gardner, first in Chapelton and then in Kingston, was a pioneer in this enterprise. The model was the British Mechanics Institutes, a development to meet the growing aspirations of British working class men and women for more than elementary education. Gardner's Jamaican version, Mutual Improvement Societies, offered weekly meetings, monthly lectures and a library to its members. An annual fee of 8/- was required and 2/6 for each lecture. Since the majority of the population could not produce the weekly pence for their children's schooling only the very successful upwardly mobile could have afforded such a membership; yet Gardner recruited 60 members at his opening meeting at Chapelton and claimed significant increases thereafter. The general nature of the mutual improvement programme can be deduced from the topics of the first four lectures which were:

	Lecturers	Subjects
Lecture 1	T.H. Clark	On Mutual Improvement
Lecture 2	Dr Smith	Composition of the Atmosphere
Lecture 3	W. Gardner	Astronomy (with magic lantern)
Lecture 4	Rector of Clarendon	The Literary History of the Bible[27]

These were clearly the somewhat esoteric, disconnected topics in the category of "useful information" so dear to the mutual improvement endeavours of Victorian England. If understood they could be stimulating sessions for a determined minority in Chapelton seeking educational betterment by any means available. The sessions would also have their attraction as social occasions and meeting places, just as did the Sunday services. What they were not was progressive further education.

The missing link for able Jamaicans was a bridge between the limited elementary schools and such college training as the religious bodies were able to sustain for any purpose, religious or secular. Since the concept of secondary education or "a sort of high schools" had in fact been formulated in the first postemancipation years, it is surprising that the missionary bodies did not apparently consider the feasibility of secondary schools earlier than they eventually did. The Methodists had not even embarked on a ministerial training school by the 1860s. The BMS, Presbyterian, Moravian missions and the CMS had set up their training schools for specific needs in missionary terms. The desirability of general further education for the mass of the population was limited to the individual enterprises in mutual improvement societies in the towns.

Duncan Fletcher, critical of his predecessor's mutual improvement society in Chapelton, did open a school for "higher education" in the town in 1862. It was for promising pupils from the day schools and for the children of families who regarded themselves as socially superior to the day schools; in short the Clarendon enterprise was a Jamaican version of the middle class schools currently developing in the United Kingdom. It targeted the most aspiring products of the day schools as well as those who no doubt regarded themselves as the new elite of Chapelton.[28]

The other notable champion for a secondary school in Jamaica was the young Methodist missionary, Enos Nuttall, newly arrived in 1862. Indeed a reproof for independent initiative in the matter may well have been one of the several reasons for his subsequent transfer to the ministry of the Established Church. Methodist Chairman, Jonathon Edmondson, was delighted with his new colleague in Kingston whom he described as "a Christian, a scholar, a man of business and a very acceptable preacher". Reviving his own idea for Methodist theological training in Jamaica, Edmondson assembled a class of twelve young men for instruction by Nuttall.[29] Nuttall himself favoured the idea of a grammar school. Whether or not through his persuasion, the District Meeting of 1864 did resolve to ask the WMMS whether they would consider a grant, to be matched in Jamaica, to buy land for the purpose.[30]

Enos Nuttall offended some of his colleagues by writing independently to the Society to press for the granting of the request. The letter coordinated all the arguments for a grammar school in the educational provision of the denomination. The day schools were essentially *elementary*; there was no place where a Methodist youth could get even enough education to prepare "for taking the lowest department of an ordinary mercantile establishment, or for becoming a druggist's apprentice". Protestant, Roman Catholic, Jewish and unsectarian schools existed, but they only led to the loss of Methodist youth; Nuttall could have added that these private schools were not intended for the elementary school graduates. A grammar school, he concluded, was the only hope in developing "an intelligent and vigorous lay agency". It was also, in his opinion, the essential first step for training a local ministry.[31]

It was to be some years more before resources were found for the development of the denominational secondary schools. By the 1860s, however, the need for a provision beyond the elementary schools was at last generally recognised. An educated, intelligent laity in all walks of life was at least as important as the hitherto small programmes for training Jamaican teachers and pastors. Enough of the products of Calabar, Fairfield, Montego Bay, Ridgemount and indeed Mico, had adopted occupations other than teaching and preaching to demonstrate that general secondary education was a greater aspiration than specific training. The postemancipation generations now sought resources for aspirations leading to a middle class status in the progressive pressure for personal security and social prestige. Such outcomes were achieved by a minority which kept its faith with the European led churches. The struggle for access to limited secondary education when it came was a new phase in the development of denominational schools.

Defeated by lack of resources either from Britain or from their Jamaican followers, the religious bodies failed adequately to provide the elementary education which had been seen as the bedrock of their task in establishing a moral and religious population in the postemancipation years. Having substantially lost the initiative in popular education, they turned their attention to training and schools for the further education of a small minority. This provided the denominations with a Jamaican leadership, and eventually contributed to the growth of a Jamaican middle class, but the achievement was far from the original missionary intention. It could be argued that by the end of the nineteenth century denominational education had done more to divide the country by class, and by colour, than it had ever done to attend to the improvement of the population at large. Increasingly an impoverished population wandered in search of work and formed city ghettoes. The economically marginal groups gave up any aspiration for schooling soon after the first postemancipation euphoria. Those who could afford to pay the small fees and dress their children to attend school became the minority. For those men who completed their elementary education, Mico, the undenominational college, was open to very small numbers. Whether they became teachers or not they were relatively isolated in their communities and sought for ways and means of bettering themselves at home and abroad.

Formal education as the essential first step in converting the population to Christian membership and morality had a strictly limited effect. Those who sent their children to school were either already converted or were simply using the only educational opportunity available; the pupils saw the schools as an integral part of social mobility, not as a preliminary to church membership, nor even as religious education. The same attitude would apply to denominational secondary schools as they developed. Without intending to do so the religious bodies in their schools provided a route to social advancement for a limited and determined minority. Eastwood, McLean, Atkinson and hundreds of others, accepted the resource, but adapted its advantages to promote their own initiatives in life.

Promotion of Free Villages

The second great attraction of missionary Christianity in the postmancipation years was the missionaries' involvement in the creation of free villages. The term itself seems to have been adopted by Phillippo when setting up Sligoville in St Catherine. Other missionaries followed the lead by begging and borrowing funds to buy land to sell back in lots to ex-slave purchasers, with deferred payment arrangements. They retained plots for chapels, mission houses and schools for the villages, thus making a commercial venture also a missionary thrust. The enabling activities of, particularly BMS, missionaries in the formation of free villages, was a strong postemancipation promotion of dissenting congregations.

This was another important instance of missionary and ex-slave purposes coinciding in the early years of emancipation. What has sometimes been called the flight from the estates was in fact a departure forced on the ex-slaves by the arbitrary activities of proprietors and their attorneys in charging unreasonable rents for estate cottages and provision grounds, and evicting ex-slaves at will. The highest aspiration of the newly free was no doubt to own land; the process was accelerated by their treatment on the estates in the first year of emancipation. Phillippo claimed that there were 150-200 free villages when he wrote in 1843; he also claimed that whereas there had only been 2,114 freeholders in the island in 1838 there were 7,340 in 1840, well over a threefold increase in the first two years of freedom.[32] Knibb, in a speech on a visit to England in 1845, quoted the previous year's census figures to show that 19,000 ex-slaves had by then bought land to build cottages.[33] Most of this early development was in the western parishes of St James, Hanover, Trelawny and in St Ann, St Mary and St Thomas-in-the-Vale, all parishes with long established BMS

European Missionary Christianity

and/or WMMS stations.[34] All missions continued to strengthen their influence where they were either the mobilisers or participants in the establishment of free villages.

The villages of this period were named after British supporters of emancipation, including established authorities such as Victoria, Normanby, Vale Lionel, with Brougham and other leaders of the anti-slavery campaign – Wilberforce, Clarkson, Buxton, Harvey, Sturge. Names of the cottages in the villages, on the other hand, expressed the deep personal sentiments of those who had marked their freedom by obtaining their own homes. Phillippo listed several cottage names which speak for themselves: Content, Pleasant Hill, Happy Hut, Free Come, Happy Grove, Jane's Delight, Save Rent, A Little of me Own, Thank God to See it.[35]

The missionaries did not, as has sometimes been implied, connive in a flight from estate labour. What they in fact assisted was the departure of free men and women from exploitative situations on the estates. The first intention was not to withdraw labour from the sugar industry, but to give the worker a secure home of his own, land for the cultivation of his food crops and a free choice of employer. William Knibb, a prime mover in enabling the establishment of free villages in Trelawny, was particularly concerned that freedom should mean the right to choose an employer; he did not advocate abandoning estate work so long as fair wages were offered.[36] The continuing decline of sugar production and consequent loss of employment on the estates was not the choice of sugar workers, nor of their pastors.[37]

Those free villages which were promoted by the missionaries in the early 1840s tended to develop as denominational enclaves.[38] Land was reserved for a chapel, a school and a mission house. With and without grants and loans from parent societies in Britain the village settlers built lime kilns, cut timber, transported stones and other materials to erect the finest chapels they could contrive, on British architectural models. They then expected the mission to provide a resident pastor and/or schoolmaster to attend to their spiritual and educational needs. While resources were available, the members accepted the responsibility of supporting both the pastor and the schoolmaster, with their usually large families, by membership dues and school fees respectively. An ordained minister who could conduct baptisms, marriages and funerals, and who could administer the Lord's Supper was regarded as highly important to those free villagers who had provided premises for those activities in their midst. When a few years later resident missionaries were not appointed, or worse were withdrawn for lack of financial support, there were strong protests from chapel stewards and members who increasingly petitioned the home societies on their own behalf.[39] They not infrequently threatened to turn alternatively to heathenism, the native Baptists or the Established Church if their requests were not met.

Perhaps the most utopian description of the "Christian village" was that of the LMS missionary Robert Jones, stationed in Chapelton. At the request of some of his members in 1840 he borrowed enough money to buy a failed property three miles from the town. He sold 180 acres in small lots and named the settlement Mount Providence. He rejoiced in now having before him "a large peaceful and prosperous Christian Village"; the deserted property had become "a garden of the Lord". Other planters in due course sold wasteland to extend the village and Jones now had 500 souls "within hearing of our bell".[40] The missionary had secured his Christian village; his members had access to his chapel and school for their families while they built up their status as freeholders. It was a mutual, if not perhaps an entirely coincident, benefit.

Not all the free villages started with missionary assistance remained the Christian enclaves seen by Robert Jones. Buchner, for instance, said in 1854 that the Moravians now regretted two experimental villages started by them in Beaufort and Beaumont; many unprincipled persons had in fact obtained the land and rejected the Moravian image of a Christian community.[41] This is unlikely to have been an isolated case over the years, particularly when the missionary presence could not be maintained. A missionary in Grateful Hill five years later complained that land "is the passion that lays all other duties under tribute"; he lamented that his large community of recent freeholders were far too preoccupied with trying to exploit their investment to maintain chapel observances or the education of their children.[42] As times became harder economic pressures in many settlements outwieghed the desire to support chapel and school as status symbols.

The majority of free villages were secured without missionary help. Particularly in parishes where missions had not been strong before emancipation, such as Clarendon, Manchester and St Catherine, many ex-slaves bought land directly with their own savings. This trend continued as more and more sugar estates failed and their proprietors sold or rented land in small lots. Many such settlements in the 1840s at first tried to emulate the missionary supported villages by having resident ministers and school teachers to lend new opportunities and prestige to their communities. The missionary resources could in no way meet the demand, particularly as the settlements of free holders became more dispersed over the island and more remote even from existing stations. This did not mean, as the missionaries told their headquarters, that the scattered people were abandoned to heathenism. It meant that they formed their own groups, mainly termed Baptist, and substantially expanded Afro-Jamaican Christian activities amongst a growing population.[43]

Decline of Missionary Christianity

By the mid 1840s the missionaries were distressed by an already perceptible decline in their influence. John Clarke, Baptist missionary in Brown's Town and promoter of the three free villages, Sturge Town, Clarksonville and Buxton, described his disappointment in the following way:

> How different now is the life of a Minister in Jamaica to that of a Missionary a few years ago. Then it was all happiness – almost unmingled joy. Wherever one went multitudes came flocking to hear the good news. Almost every Monday I would have 20 to 100 anxious enquirers – Baptisms large and frequent – scarcely any exclusions – all at peace in the Mission. Now congregations are as good as ever – but comparatively few come forward enquiring what must we do to be saved – Baptisms are few and far between – cases of discipline are numerous and painful, and our missionary band is rent asunder.[44]

The manifestations of waning influence were clear. Attendance at preaching services remained large where they could be reached and where Sunday best clothes, if not finery, could be afforded. The Sunday service was a social institution. What declined early was membership and the large classes of "enquirers" and "candidates" preparing for formal admission to the chapels and churches. The missionaries at first put it down to their own lack of resources and implored their societies to send reinforcements. Their letters home described how impossible it was to reach the scattered population thirsting for Christian conversion.

Obviously no European missionary religion could reach districts where it had no representatives, and the missionaries were indeed stretched well beyond islandwide effectiveness. Burchell, for example, at one stage had twelve preaching stations connected with the BMS chapel in Montego Bay.[45] William Hamm, the first European Methodist missionary actually to be ordained in Jamaica, itemised the activities of his four probationary years. He had served in eight circuits to supply emergency vacancies, had been thrown from his horse sixteen times, had travelled 8,320 miles, had spoken at auxiliary missionary meetings in all the parishes, had preached about 832 times and, he concluded with regret, had read only 110 volumes. Furthermore, he claimed, "If I had possessed talents I should have been required to give advice on almost every subject relating to medicine, law and various trades, besides that of directing the minds of the people to the Lamb of God which taketh away the sins of the World."[46] This account more than suggests that there was a considerable difference in the perception of the missionary role between the pastors themselves, coming with a reforming zeal to convert a heathen people, and the ex-slaves whom they sought to convert. The latter retained a great appreciation of evangelistic sermons and addresses coupled with the confidence that the preachers could also deal with the multiple practical problems of the new free state. According to dispirited missionaries, the spiritual benefits of the Christian religion were the priority of a minority only, and that mainly consisting of the older people forever grateful for their delivery from slavery. Younger generations were more concerned to find satisfaction in this world rather than consolation for lack of it in the next. "Worldliness" and "lack of spirituality" were criticisms regularly levelled at the postemancipation population by the European missionaries who had sought to guide the values of the free society.

Where at the beginning of the 1840s missionaries might reasonably have thought that they were well embarked on the wholesale conversion of Jamaica to European Christianity, the progress of the decade disillusioned them on that score. Reverend David King, on a visit from the Scottish Missionary Society in 1850, was uncompromising in his view that former missionaries had greatly overrated their success and that Jamaica still remained very much a field for missionary endeavour. "Why this is called a Christian country, we cannot tell", he declared, "unless a loose and general profession of religion be the reason."[47]

It was the "loose and general profession of religion" that disturbed the missionaries most. Even their faithful chapel attenders no longer apparently repented for their many sins or prepared themselves for salvation. The prevalent failings were, in missionary opinion, covetousness, a love of finery, litigiousness, quarrelsomeness, addiction to rum shops and of course the "carnal sins" and "fornication" amongst those who "heard" but did not follow the preachers. Perhaps even more disturbingly for the missionaries there was a growing disposition to turn to the native Baptists, certainly wherever the missions could not provide a resident preacher or a school. Former leaders who sustained the preaching stations with little support from the missionaries often became independent preachers taking their followers with them. Not only were the European pastors failing to fulfil their original purposes, they were losing ground both as proselytisers and also as effective influences on the flocks they did maintain.

The explanations for the decline given by the people at large were obviously different. For one thing they were less concerned with denominational distinctions than their European pastors. There was a good deal of switching from one to another. By and large the missions which had a resident minister, a schoolmaster and premises to contain them gained the local membership. Attendance at services largely depended on which preacher was available at different stations on different Sundays; an ordained minister, regardless of denomination and all things being equal, drew the crowds. The Established Church, now with its own missionary activities, gained recruits, not least because it was less searching into the private morality of its candidates than the deacons and other leaders of the dissenting chapels. Furthermore, financed by the Colonial Government and their vestries, the churches did not charge the dues, or the school fees, required by missions. Where the choice was available, transfer to the Established Church was ironically an alternative threat to that of joining the native Baptists by those expelled from the dissenting chapels for various forms of backsliding.

The financial requirements were almost certainly the main cause of the decline of the mission chapels. By the mid forties only a declining minority of the working population was even modestly secure, and few had realistic hopes of becoming so. The steady decline of the sugar estates led to unemployment or at best drastically low wages for seasonal work only. The House of Assembly's immigration schemes brought in Indian, African and Chinese workers as competition further to reduce the chances of living wages for Jamaican workers. Droughts and hurricanes were frequent, ruining food crops for local consumption and attacking small farmer export crops such as pimento. These were the standby of the aspiring ex-slaves who had joined the mission chapels in the first postemancipation years, and who could thus afford in good times to support chapels and pay for their children's schooling. Destitution and even starvation increasingly became the realistic prospect before which aspirations for social betterment, including chapel membership, faded. Men, and to a lesser extent women, were wandering the island, and beyond, in search of employment. Young people increasingly left their families to set up homes with each other, both in the towns and in country districts. This was not the scenario for the stable chapel communities envisaged, for instance, in the free village movement. The socioeconomic decline described by Edward Underhill, Secretary of the BMS, after his visit to Jamaica in 1859 was apparent by the mid 1840s.[48] The vision of a respectable, hard-working peasantry guided by Victorian dissenting chapel values largely vanished in face of the harsh realities.

The missionary societies in Britain were also overextended by their growing endeavours in Africa and Asia. Their missionaries in Jamaica were charged to organise their own support from the supposedly prospering peasantry which, with British generosity, had emerged from slavery and who should now be able to afford their own chapels. Not only did the home missions decline to underwrite future costs they also took no responsibility for heavy chapel debts incurred in the overoptimistic years immediately following emancipation. The missionaries agonised over their predicaments in the Jamaican field. Their flocks neither understood nor effectively shared them.

A faithful minority did their best to find funds to maintain their pastors, and they personally appealed to British missionary societies not to abandon them. The majority simply avoided commitments that they could not meet in the costs of joining classes leading to full membership of the chapels. Attendance at the Sunday service, with the best available preacher, regardless of denomination, was the extent of most missionary led Christian observance, and even this was in decline when people were unable to present a respectable appearance for the occasion.

Most of the chapels had been built with some subsidy from the British missionary society which "owned" them. A House of Assembly grant was finally awarded in 1837 to restore the dissenting chapels which had been destroyed by the Colonial Church Union in 1832. It was used to help build new chapels twice the size of those they replaced. A European-style chapel with a British subsidy added to local contributions in cash, materials and labour, was the hallmark of postemancipation self-expression in many a community. When these buildings in due course required extension or repair, questions arose as to their ownership. The missionaries were certain that they were missionary society property, and warned that local lenders would call in their loans at short notice, if it were thought to be otherwise.[49] William Knibb and John Clarke could not understand why the BMS did not raise loans on the security of the chapels in Jamaica.[50] Jamaican stewards, deacons and leaders increasingly saw the matter differently, particularly when the British societies declined to help with chapel debts and maintenance costs. Assertions about Jamaican ownership of the chapels thereafter accompanied most petitions and protests to the British society, whatever the specific grievance presented in each.

The decline in missionary influence included the loss of leaders who had hitherto been the bedrock of conversion to missionary Christianity. The reasons were in fact predictable. The majority of BMS and WMMS followers saw their European pastors on an average once a month, in many cases only once in two or three months. The continuum of their worship and moral superintendence rested with their local leaders, ranging from illiterate fellow workers to the teacher/catechists where they were appointed. Since the people were also abandoning classes and membership which required fees they saw even less of the visiting missionaries. As the impetus was locally maintained it was a short step to set up an independent religious group, of native Baptists or independent Methodists, under strong local "parsons", deacons and leaders. Furthermore, since the native churches had no coordinating islandwide organisation, they allowed for much local self-expression and application to the actual concerns of the people. This must have seemed a much more realistic religious allegiance than a tenuous link with a European mission chapel where in any case social and financial requirements could not be met. The European Christian decline was undoubtedly accompanied by a native Christian advance.

Two major disputes occurred within the European missions themselves and caused breakaway groups.[51] Allegations of colour prejudice against some of his older colleagues finally led to the resignation in 1847 of the Methodist Chairman, Thomas Pennock. Promoted by Jordon, Osborn and other influential coloured members of the Kingston circuit, he agreed to lead a breakaway group known, at least by the WMMS missionaries, as Pennockites. They were for some time influential in Kingston, St Andrew, St Mary, St Thomas-in-the-East and St Ann in particular. Perhaps most significantly in the long run the breakaway served as a precedent for other, native-led independent Methodist groups.

The Baptist fallout was more localised in Spanish Town where for some six years in the 1840s an acrimonious dispute arose between the supporters of the established missionary, James Phillippo, and the followers of his young co-pastor, Thomas Dowson. What started as a disagreement over the status and duties of the "co-pastor", after Phillippo had been away in Britain on a long leave, developed into a major ministerial power struggle enthusiastically promoted by the lay supporters on both sides. Events included Dowson's exclusion from the Baptist burial ground during a funeral service which he was conducting, the seizure of the chapel by his followers in retaliation and the subsequent closure of the chapel for nearly three years while the High Court of Chancery decided, not only who the chapel belonged to, but also who was the rightful pastor in charge. The final decision in favour of Phillippo, largely because of his long standing rather than for his popularity, led to a sizeable secession by the membership and the setting up of an independent Baptist chapel in Spanish Town, with Dowson in charge.

These two very public disputes in critical years for the British missions did little to enhance missionary prestige in Jamaican eyes and certainly provoked sustained claims by chapel officers and the membership that they were responsible for decision making in their own chapels. In both cases the loyalties of the missionaries were divided and much time was spent on internal issues which was needed in the field if they were to hold their ground, let alone extend their influence. Above all, Jamaican opinion ran strong in both disputes, and the influential majority finally went in both cases with the secessionist group. These strong sentiments probably hardly reached the mass of the population beyond Kingston, Spanish Town and the capital towns of the neighbouring parishes, but they set another precedent, added to the long-standing native Baptist tradition, for Jamaican led Christian groups.

European missionaries on the ground obviously had different individual perceptions of their own effectiveness during what can now be seen as a period of decline. A Methodist chairman of the long experience of Jonathan Edmondson could read the times more perceptively than most.[52] During a series of islandwide pastoral visits to Methodist circuits in 1849 he described the economic failure which threatened the people. He commented on the lack of employment except at very low wages, paid only at crop time, the failure to pay even these wages where they were due and the breakdown of small farmer production after a series of natural disasters. Edmondson confirmed that members lacked the funds to support the missionaries at their stations. He noted also that leaders were withdrawing from mission service as they left their districts in search of paid employment; others resigned because they were no longer provided with travelling or subsistence expenses by the missions. An increasingly impoverished people needed their own resources for survival. Since the missionaries could not alone maintain pastoral care in the scattered prayer stations there was considerable "unwillingness to support the Gospel". If pressed for contributions Edmondson found that even chapel members threatened to leave Methodism and routinely offered, on the one hand, the Established Church and, on the other, the native Baptists as their available alternatives. As both were anathema to the dissenting missionaries Edmondson was reporting a devastating picture of missionary loss by 1849.[53]

It must have been clear to all the British missionaries in Jamaica by the end of the 1840s that they were not to be the agents for wholesale conversion to Christianity in the foreseeable future. Dwindling support from Britain and failing resources in Jamaica ensured that they could at best save existing chapels and stations; consistent proselytism in new districts was now impossible. The European missionary had become a minister for a minority who could sustain him, and his family, in a lifestyle which, however reduced, required European standards in the domestic sphere.

Similarly, the teacher/catechists who maintained the day schools and the alternative Sunday preaching were too few in number to reach a widely scattered population; they too did little more than save the existing congregations. They were not the effective religious recruiting officers that the earlier deacons and leaders had been. Increasingly the successful products of the day schools, often followed by training at Mico College, were ambitious for better, or at least better paid, employment at home and abroad. The lay chapel leadership, for example, was observed again to decline during the first major emigration for work in the 1850s.

The perennial missionary criticism of what they regarded as lack of spirituality and abiding immorality amongst the Jamaican people, must have made them appear unsympathetic to much of the population. Despite their recognition of the people's hardships they made no concessions in their constant criticism of their prevailing lifestyle and expelled rather than redeemed the backsliders. The chapels had promoted a culture of respectability and morality; when these values were not maintained by an increasingly impoverished and marginalised population their missionaries saw the outcome as spiritual and moral weakness. Only a few, mainly young, missionaries took to early morning and open air preaching where standards of dress could be ignored; some also valued home visiting above traditional preaching for pastoral effectiveness; but only a minority tried to adjust to the restraints of poverty. Notable among these were the small number of Jamaican missionaries who tended to maintain the proselytising role longer than their European colleagues.[54]

Sadly aware of their own decline in influence the missionaries still sustained their loyalty to the labouring classes. They invariably disputed strong suggestions that the ex-slaves were idle or lazy. They recognised the dire effects of low, often unpaid, wages. They opposed the House of Assembly's immigration schemes as a gross waste of public money aimed at reducing still further remuneration for sugar workers. All these matters were raised in letters to the home societies, but seldom raised publicly in Jamaica. The one issue on which the missionaries did let their collective views be known was the ruinous effect of the British Sugar Duties Equalisation Act. They lobbied strongly for their societies in Britain to attack the British Government on the subject.[55] They were not in fact moved only by the potential ruin of the planters, who were presenting their own case forcefully. The threat to missionary activity lay rather with the consequent ruin of the labourers as even seasonal employment in sugar diminished. In this respect missionaries in Jamaica found common cause with the continued anti-slavery lobby in Britain. Missionary opinion on public distress, however, may not have been well understood by their followers who in their destitution were more immediately aware of their chapels' regular demands for dues and fees. The missionaries strengthened their reputation for money-seeking by their remarks on their own lack of security and the possibility of having to abandon their missions.

There was a surge of renewed interest in the chapels during the epidemics of the 1850s, which between them reached all areas of the island. As there was only one public medical officer for each parish there was virtually no attention available for the afflicted. Several missionaries provided drugs and set up pharmacies in their mission houses, where their wives and daughters worked tirelessly to alleviate and control the sickness. All missionaries visited the sick and buried the dead. Wheeler, the LMS missionary in Kingston, reported that he had visited some 2,500 cholera cases and about 300 were attending his home dispensary daily.[56] The Methodist, Stedman, at Grateful Hill commented that people expected ministers to provide the support in epidemics which used to be provided in estate hospitals during slavery.[57] The LMS missionary at Ridgemount, Mandeville, personally vaccinated 1,500 of his local followers against smallpox.[58] William Holdsworth claimed that he was doctor and nurse as well as pastor to his flock in Savanna-la-Mar. He further expressed the opinion that his activities during the epidemic were "populating heaven with precious souls and in the hand of their Heavenly Master are sending Gems to adorn the diadem of their Redeemer on the great day of 'the feast'".[59] Such an exaltation over the sequel to a dire visitation must have met with a mixed reception in the town.

Most of the dissenting missionaries held the view that the epidemics of the early fifties were sent by God to chasten a wicked people and bring them back to the chapels. "Alas we have seen judgement upon judgement", wrote John Vaz, one of the Jamaican missionaries.[60] Many thought that the visitation had brought more good than evil in its wake. "The awful scourge . . . has been blessed to many people in this part of the island," declared a missionary in Yallahs.[61] The veteran, James Rowden, described how the chapel at Lime Savanna was now bursting at the seams on Sundays and that 200 people were now applying for admission in Vere "so deeply are they impressed with the brevity of life and the necessity of preparing for Eternity".[62] Another Jamaican, Robert Johnson, shared his European colleagues' conclusion that "the rod had not been laid upon us in vain". He reported that "many careless souls" in Spanish Town had returned and many were seeking marriage.[63]

The truth of the matter no doubt lay in Robert Johnson's observation of "the many careless souls" who returned in times of tribulation. That it was the lapsed membership which for a time returned to the fold was confirmed by Martin Young in Montego Bay, who observed that the mortality of one in eight or ten in the town had had a great effect on the piety of the members and had drawn back previous hearers; however, he recognised, "the masses of ungodly people around us are alarmed and paralysed but only a very few are found enquiring after God".[64] It is a fair presumption that the "ungodly people" in the western town were in fact flocking to their Myal doctor for medical attention and/or to their native Baptist groups for religious solace.

It is apparent that the experience of widespread epidemics in the 1850s for a time restored the congregations in the missionary chapels. There is little evidence, however, that "the scourges" widened the missionary influence by reaching new and marginalised groups in the society. Because the missionaries still did not recognise, and so did not discuss, their popular religious rivals, it can only be inferred that native Christian and Myal groups were also boosted during, and because of, these years of tribulation and disease. In short the missionary chapels had a brisk new period of recovery; it was not otherwise an expansion of missionary achievement.

Some ground was lost to the European missionaries in interdenominational criticism which does not, however, appear to have concerned the Jamaican following very much. During the early postemancipation years representations were made to the BMS in London by CMS, LMS and Presbyterian missionaries in Jamaica.[65] Their objections were that BMS missionaries were baptising their candidates too freely and admitting members without either due preparation or subsequent supervision; in consequence, maintained the critics, BMS members had not abandoned their heathen African practices and were thus degrading Christianity in Jamaica.

The BMS missionaries denied that they lacked control and supervision of their membership; they also declared that surviving superstitions were declining steadily.[66] The nondenominational LMS missionaries, who were nevertheless strict Protestant evangelists in any case, may well have been genuinely shocked at mass baptisms and the power of the Baptist leaders in their remote stations. They themselves were so exacting in their doctrinal requirements for admission that many enquirers departed from them, after years of waiting, because they despaired of ever being qualified for LMS membership. On the whole the grievance against the BMS missionaries was an envious one because they were at first better supported from Britain with building costs to expand their stations and schools more rapidly than their fellow dissenting missionaries. They also received capital to buy land more readily than the others and so were able to associate themselves with the free village movement most speedily. The BMS missionaries undoubtedly preached the same moral and religious values as their other Protestant colleagues; they may, however, have been more subject to fluctuating allegiance between the BMS chapels and native Baptist groups. This may have made them appear more associated with Afro-Jamaican Baptist activities than they in fact were.

The other target for interdenominational rivalry was the Established Church. Because it was supported by the Colonial Government it could provide churches and chapels of ease without payment of dues by the congregation, and schools without the payment of fees. One of William Knibb's main reasons for promoting the black freeholder vote to the House of Assembly was that he wanted them to pressure for the disestablishment of the Anglican Church in Jamaica. All dissenting missionaries objected to Anglican rivalry which did to some extent draw off their membership, particularly in the towns. The more prosperous and established coloured families tended to join the Anglican churches where they had earlier supported the Methodists. It is reasonable to infer that they sought a social distinction in distancing themselves from the newly free black and coloured aspirants to missionary respectability who in the main stayed with the dissenting missions.

Another grievance against the Established Church was that it was, in the words of the Jamaican missionary Alexander Lindo, "an asylum for the expelled". Backsliders condemned for immorality, lying and quarreling certainly threatened to transfer themselves to the Established Church, which was generally thought to be more lenient in these matters; they no doubt at least attended Anglican services when challenged in the chapels, whether or not they became communicant members. It would appear that the curates and catechists of the Established Church were more active as preachers and teachers than as moral supervisors of their flocks. This, with the absence of regular dues and fees, led to a steadily increasing membership. As one new recruit put it, "It is the same God there, and we shall have no money to throw."[67]

Finally, the first Bishops of Jamaica tended to develop High Church practices which caused Edmondson to fulminate against the spread of contemporary Puseyism from England. The Jamaican congregations, however, may well have enjoyed rituals and symbolism which were discouraged in the chapels. Dissenting missionaries maintained that Anglican followers were not instructed in the Christian religion. One critic even asserted that some did not know who Jesus Christ was. "Me neber hear of Him" they are reported as saying.[68] Most of the interdenominational rivalry occurred in the towns or in growing settlements, and was provoked by inroads, usually Baptist, onto territory formerly serviced by other missions. Phillippo's intervention from Spanish Town in the rapidly growing village of Porus, for example, was particularly resented by the LMS mission because the Baptist missionary sought his following by representing the nondenominational LMS group established there as "half Christians".[69]

The consequences of denominational competition were well demonstrated at Grateful Hill where by 1859 there were fourteen places of Christian worship within a seven mile radius of the settlement. They were listed as follows: two Wesleyan, two Baptist, three native Baptist, two American Mission (Congregationalist), three Associationists (Pennockites), one Established Church, one Roman Catholic. It is important to note that of the fourteen centres of worship six were independent groups formed in the country, namely the three native Baptist and the three Pennockite chapels. It is also significant to record that this information was contained in Missionary Holdsworth's letter complaining that the people were in any case so preoccupied with their problems of land development that they had little time for worship or education of any kind.[70] The local interdenominational excess of rivalry does not appear to have concerned its subjects.

In the more remote rural stations the resources of each mission were too small to threaten each other to any great extent. Indeed there was a good deal of cooperation and mutual assistance in country districts, where missionaries tried to deploy their scattered stations for maximum accessibility rather than to compete with each other. They also tried to supplement each others' efforts as for example in the united prayer meetings conducted in Brown's Town between the veteran Baptist John Clark, the socially concerned Methodist, William Tyson and the Rev Harry Cahusac of the Established Church.[71] Ministers regularly gave hospitality to each other on their travels; they attended each others' chapel and school events; they preached and lectured in each others' premises and conducted, or assisted at, ordinations and funerals of fellow missionaries and their family members. Above all, they frequently combined in the presentations at the long, popular and islandwide auxiliary missionary meetings to raise money for overseas missions. In effect, despite reservations about certain differing denominational practices, European missionaries were closer to each other in their mutual interests than they probably were to the majority of their congregations and certainly to the mass of the population at large.

There was undoubtedly in some quarters a latent feeling of resentment against European ministers, clergy and missionaries, who assumed their superiority in denominational hierarchies; their attitudes sometimes resembled those of their fellow white British, the planting interests and the colonial officials. It was not only their chapel stewards, assistant missionaries and teacher/catechists who were often frustrated; the black preachers were also wont to emphasise that the European missionary was a white man whose final political allegiance was to the authorities in another country.

The views expressed by the joint memorial against the Sugar Duties Equalisation Act of "the Ministers of all denominations" in 1852 somewhat illustrated ministerial priority concerns in public affairs. As secretary to the group the Presbyterian missionary, James Watson, explained that they had combined because they were concerned for "the fate of this important colony and the future well-being of its emancipated inhabitants". They were making a unanimous effort "to arrest, if possible the evils that threaten to overwhelm the country".[72] After a lengthy introduction stating the long held missionary position that they would never interfere in public affairs except where these threatened their work, the memorialists claimed that they were now so jeopardised, and that "in the threatened ruin of the agricultural and commercial interests of this country our own usefulness and ministrations are involved". Unless the differential duties were restored between the produce of the free cultivator in Jamaica and foreign slave grown sugars "the privations already sustained by the planter, the labours of the Ministers of religion and the costly philanthropy of the Mother Country in effecting emancipation will be abortive".[73]

The attitudes and priorities of this memorial are revealing. The memorialists' injured parties were in order of presentation, first the planters, then English anti-slavery activists and finally themselves. The problems of the free cultivator, when finally discussed, were described as the loss of missionary attention rather than as the loss of employment and consequent dire distress in face of the steady decline of the sugar industry. The memorial's arguments on behalf of the working population are hardly a plea for the social development of the population at large. In the event of continued decline of sugar, the memorial predicted:

> The cultivation of the estates and the religious and educational institutions of the island must be simultaneously abandoned; while the masses of our population will inevitably retrograde to a state of barbarism and crime, worse than that from which, under the grace of God, and by the charity of a great nation, they have been rescued, and the return of which it is our earnest care to deprecate and avert.[74]

The emphases and tone of this document show, in the first place, that the ministers related themselves with colonial interests, at home and abroad, rather than with the Jamaican people in their distress. Secondly, the failure even to mention in the context the widespread problems of unemployment, low wages and consequent impoverishment suggests a considerable distancing from the real concerns of "the masses of our population". A comparison with a stipendiary magistrate's report on St Thomas-in-the-Vale only two years later shows a striking contrast in his perception of the people's problems. The magistrate attributed their difficulties both to the progressive failure of the sugar estates and to the growing isolation of the freeholders' settlements; in these circumstances he foresaw "the rapidly approaching importance which must very soon attach to these small settlements and their yeomanry of possessors".[75] There was a striking difference in attitude between the special magistrate's "yeomanry" and the missionaries' population which "will inevitably retrograde into barbarism and crime". The contrast is made because it highlights the missionaries' preoccupation with the challenges of their immediate postemancipation task long after the free society had developed grave new problems. It is little wonder that the chapels retained an elderly constituency who remembered the euphoria of emancipation, but increasingly lost the younger generations who had not experienced slavery although they still associated themselves with the aspirations for social mobility that accompanied the abolition.

The missionaries deplored the absence of young people, including the products of the day schools, from the chapels and their free association in sexual relationships. They noted the ever increasing mobility of the young in search of work, subsistence and simply peer group mutual solace. The Kingston pastors wrote periodically about a depressed and often criminal underclass growing in the city, entirely outside religious influences. In the countryside gangs of young people wandered in search of a livelihood and added to the growing incidence of praedial larceny. The shocking conditions later revealed in the *Royal Commission Report on the Juvenile Population* of 1879 were already documented by the missionaries a quarter of a century earlier. Yet they did little to confront the situation; they deplored the results rather than tackled the causes. The generations born after emancipation provided not a heathen mass to be converted to Christianity, but a marginal, depressed population, to the majority of whom neither African nor European religion apparently mattered much.

The missionaries should have realised that their part in the British emancipation movement was no longer a recommendation when as early as 1845 they could not persuade their members to contribute to the testimonial on the death of Thomas Powell Buxton. The Methodist Richard Hornabrook, himself the son of a missionary, frankly declared that "*Quashy* does not manifest that gratitude for favours received which we have a right to expect from him." No longer, he reported, did crowds attend commemorative services on 1 August. "The day is coming," Hornabrook predicted, "when the objects of Buxton's sympathy will feel unwilling to be reminded of their former degradation." He recognised as a corollary that the people no longer loved and respected their missionaries, nor their services.[76] If, as seems probable, this observation was right it must be assumed that the missionaries' continued assumption that they should be inspirational leaders because of their association with emancipation, was out of date much earlier than the majority realised. It could not outlast the painful realities of life in the free society.

Social commentators were to arise both among the Jamaican missionaries and among young British recruits appointed to the missions long after the emancipation effect was lost to the people. In the meantime most missionaries saw themselves as "ministers" of chapels with a declining congregation of the faithful and a population continuously fading into distant and inaccessible settlements or into the escape of mobility in search of work. Missionary fervour for the conversion of a population became rather a maintenance operation to provide services for those already converted to respectability and European moral standards, and able to maintain the lifestyle required to sustain their social standing.

CHAPTER 3

Jamaican Initiatives in Missionary Christianity

No good can be done by any man who opposes the will of the people.
Petition of the LMS members of Mount Zion, 1843

Most Jamaicans were converted to mission congregations by their own countrymen and women. They received the seal of ministerial admission to baptism, membership and participation in the Lord's Supper only after years of preparation by Jamaican deacons, leaders, elders, helpers, aids, according to the terminology of the different denominations. From this Jamaican leadership emerged from time to time strong assertions of independent attitudes and opinions. Sometimes this was in expressed opposition to some missionary intention; more often it was the exercise of status obtained in the chapels to influence the affairs of the community at large. It was an effective leadership role often far beyond that envisaged, or even noticed, by the missionaries. Nevertheless, when the leadership moved away or acted independently the mission stations were seriously weakened.

Probably the most productive cooperation between missionaries and chapel members occurred in that part of the early free village movement which was promoted by missionary support and loan finance. Here there was mutual benefit. Aspiring freeholders could obtain land and building materials on systems of extended payment which they could afford. The missionaries benefited by rising numbers appreciative of their support and willing to build chapels and schools as symbols of the kind of communities that they were seeking for themselves. Settlements of contented peasantry ready to work on the sugar estates and to grow their own food crops seemed assured if they had their own cottages, provision grounds, a chapel, a school and a mission house. These enclaves tended to be the preserve of one denomination, and tended to be unwelcoming to others. Missionaries were gratified by the outcome because each new village represented a new consolidated and committed station. The members had easy access to a chapel and a school for their families while they built up further status as smallholders. It was a mutual, if not an entirely corresponding, benefit in prospect.

Where the new settlements were the initiative of the free people themselves, without missionary help, they were less likely to become the preserve of any one mission. Increasingly as the villages became more scattered and remote there was no mission chapel at all. In these cases the villagers invariably formed their own groups and nominated them Baptist. European pastors often reported finding a Baptist community with no missionary to serve it. Since there was no coordinating body for the native Baptist groups their statistics are nonexistent. They were, however, constantly encountered and their cohesive strength reported by missionaries throughout the island.

The missionaries offered a model for a lifestyle which could give ex-slaves self-respect and status symbols in standards of "respectability" sustained by Christian morality. This to a considerable extent coincided with the ideas for life in freedom held by many ex-slaves themselves. It is remarkable how far people struggling to maintain themselves and their families in fact set up standards of social behaviour, including Christian worship, with little contact with the missionaries. Many of the more remote communities aspired to the "missionary culture" on their own initiative. One missionary was invited to a tea meeting in a settlement 4,000 feet up in the mountains; some people had walked ten miles to attend the function and they had raised £10 in the hope of attracting a pastor since they as yet only had a schoolmaster.[1] At a settlement near Arcadia Estate a group was holding their own prayer meeting twice a week in a wattled shelter with a simple pulpit and benches which they had constructed themselves; they had also started a graveyard nearby. As none of the group could read, a boy from a Methodist day school read for them.[2] Another community which had erected a wattle shelter for their prayer meetings did not want a European pastor until they could provide a better structure for his chapel. Whatever the missionaries thought about Jamaican religious initiatives the people obviously saw themselves as Christians, and practising ones at that.

Every mission reported herculean efforts on the part of the members in building chapels, schools and mission houses. When the home missionary societies declined to meet heavy debts incurred, particularly in towns, poor people raised large sums of money over many years to maintain the interest payments and hopefully reduce the principal. Different methods were used. Benjamin Dexter, the BMS missionary based in Stewart Town, reported £408 raised by the members in two months towards a £1,300 chapel debt at his station, more than £156 in a drought year towards a £900 commitment at Rio Bueno, and at Great River the members were putting up a chapel and a house asking only £300 from the BMS for both.[3] John Clarke at Brown's Town reported that his deacons could not raise cash but were willing to offer their houses, worth £200-£300 each, as security for local loans.[4]

Once the loan hazard had become clear plenty of chapel building was undertaken with minimal capital requirement. In Clarendon two chapels built of stone were opened on succeeding Sundays, both free of debt. They had been built in under a year by the contributions of the members, in cash and in labour, helped by "a few respectable friends".[5] At Garden Hill, an outstation in the mountains served by the Methodist missionary at Bath, the people built a chapel bringing materials from thirty miles away, the last seven miles as headloads to the top of the mountains.[6] Chairman Edmondson, on tour of the district in 1849, came upon a chapel being erected at Yallahs by impoverished people who were unable to get any paid employment.[7]

The missionaries' own efforts to raise funds were of a British variety. They begged help from individuals and congregations in Britain. They requested items of clothing and other articles to be sold at bazaars. An early begging letter from the Knibbs to a friend in Falmouth, England, listed the articles which would get a ready sale in Falmouth, Jamaica, as follows:

> Frocks, pinafores, aprons, collars, gloves, handkerchiefs, threads, tapes, bobbins, buttons, pins, needles, scissors, dishmats, baskets of all sorts, bonnets, caps, ribbons, children's clothes and toys and remnants for sewing classes.[8]

These could be articles only for the "respectable" with a cash income. Falmouth could no doubt raise such purchasers with a population containing several generations of free coloureds who had done well in business. Cash income, however, was just what was increasingly lacking to others free in whatever generation. It is hard to see, for instance, what such a gift meant in Mount Fletcher in 1849 when the missionary declared that a British contribution of articles for a bazaar had averted the bankruptcy of the chapel trustees; in the same letter he also reported that there had been deaths from starvation in the district.[9] Later that year the chairman further reported that people from Mount Fletcher were migrating to St Andrew in search of work, and changing to the Established Church to escape the chapel debt of £134; only 50 of the 500 members were now paying regular dues.[10]

In fact many of the chapels were erected and maintained in outstations without a resident missionary or even in some cases without a teacher/catechist. Chairman Edmondson pointed out that in 1833 there had been sixteen chapels in the Jamaica district; thirty years later there were sixty-one.[11] The mounting complement of chapels were the initiative of local people using money, labour and local loans to build and maintain what they then regarded as their own chapel property.

In the circumstances the stewards, leaders and concerned members of the chapels felt entitled to express their opinions both to the missionaries in the field and quite often directly to the missionary headquarters in London. Independent opinions were a long-standing tradition amongst stewards and members of the Kingston Methodist chapels; they certainly maintained it in the postemancipation years. Tired of adverse missionary comment on the quality of their spiritual religion in 1846 they addressed the home society directly. In a memorial signed by Charles Lake, the Chief Steward, they stated that the decline in the chapel income had nothing to do with any decline in their spiritual state; the true causes were, in order stated, drought, shortage of supplies, commercial distress, unemployment and sickness.[12] The members had a precise explanation of their own financial problems and did not appreciate suggestions that the quality of their religious commitment was involved.

In country areas the confrontations were usually about premises built by members. At Green Hill, for instance, where the missionary from Brown's Town only occasionally reached them, the people claimed the right to decide on the future of their own chapel when the mission wanted to sell it in hard times. Furthermore they were unable to understand why there was still a debt on the property after they had been "throwing up" for so many years. "Misunderstandings and heart-burnings" were also reported from the Tabernacle at Brown's Town and from the Stewart Town chapel members.[13] The "misunderstanding" was invariably that some members did not realise that their protracted payments were meeting only the interest charges on loans and not reducing the principal.

Probably the strongest stand of the period came from the LMS members in Morant Bay. They maintained "resistance" to a proposal that their chapel should be sold over a period of ten years. They regularly protested that they had not been consulted, and in the critical year of 1865 withheld their dues because the matter was still pending.[14] Lindo, now a missionary in Porus, who had spent many years as a successful teacher/catechist in Morant Bay, warned that the people would riot if their chapel was sold.[15] No other denomination would be allowed "to buy their property". In a resolution to the LMS, signed by two Morant Bay deacons and two from Prospect, they begged for extra time to find money for their expenses; they expressed strong indignation that their chapel might be sold to become a rum shop, a tavern or "a synagogue of Satan".[16] It is a fair assumption that the last was a reference to the local native Baptists who might have bought the premises. In fact the LMS was contemplating sale to the BMS.

There is no doubt that as the missions were increasingly required to be self-supporting, those who remained faithful to their chapels found considerable sums, not only for the buildings and their maintenance, but also for the upkeep of their pastors and their often large families. They embarked on the responsibility with pride in their independent ability to do so. This can be seen in two resolutions passed by the Morant Bay LMS members and their neighbours in Prospect in 1840. The Morant Bay congregation accepted their responsibilities in the following statement:

> That as we are now free, and as we are taught by the Word of God that it is the duty of Christian Churches to support their own Pastors, we resolve, if possible, to raise amongst ourselves the salary of our Minister from June 30, 1840, so that he shall no longer be obliged to draw on the Parent Society for this item.

The Prospect acceptance was even more strongly in the same vein:

> That we are in possession of the rights and privileges of free born citizens, for which we thank God and his Church, we will freely cooperate with you in accomplishing the pleasing duty to which you have called our attention.[17]

The distress of the faithful minority when they could not fulfil their "rights and privileges" in paying for their own pastor was intensified by the feeling that it was one of the status symbols of their free state. Great ingenuity was shown over the years in finding ways to maintain the missionaries. The LMS members at Mount Zion paid their pastor in produce and planted land for his family provisions. In one year they planted yams, cocos and plantains for the minister and his family, and corn for his horse; they also set him up in poultry for the year.[18] Some of the contributions were made individually as a member earned a little cash. A later missionary at Mount Zion described an offering of 3/- made to him with the following specifications, "for me, this 1/-; for me wife this 9d; this 9d for me eldest daughter; this 3d for me youngest, and this 1½d for me grandchild; this [presumably another 1½d] for Minister to buy book [the Bible] to send to them wild people you tell me 'bout".[19] The last item was for LMS activities in India which had been described at a recent meeting of the auxiliary missionary society. It is an interesting revelation of the impression left on the mind of a smallholder in Mount Zion, doubtless confirmed by encounters with depressed Indian immigrant workers on Clarendon estates. The personal pride of the man in contributing, however humbly, to both his pastor's upkeep and to the conversion of India is quite unmistakable.

The auxiliary missionary society meetings were a popular attraction all over the island. The missionaries initiated the auxiliary societies to assist their missions' expanding activities in all parts of the non-Christian world. For Jamaicans the spiritual needs of heathen Africa as presented by the missionaries were more often the focus of attention than those of Asia. They held largely attended annual meetings in all stations which lasted several hours while three or four missionaries gave vivid accounts of the crying needs for salvation of the heathen world. The meetings were a huge social, as well as chapel related, event and they raised quite large sums of money, even in stations which were having problems over the collection of regular dues and school fees. As early as 1845 one missionary observed that the people were very generous with funds for their premises

Jamaican Initiatives in Missionary Christianity

and for the auxiliary missionary society, but resented regular payments. "Hundreds withdraw rather than comply with the rule", he stated. This was in the year that the missionaries had failed to raise contributions for a memorial to Fowell Buxton. It would appear that large numbers of even chapel members preferred to identify themselves with the interests of their African "brothers" rather than with the memory of the British emancipator.[20]

Not only Jamaican funds, but also Jamaican missionaries were provided for the task of converting West Africans to Christianity. There were said to be twenty-three Jamaican Moravians in Accra, Gulf of Guinea, by 1843, and they "have proved themselves useful missionary colonists".[21] These were the worker missionaries promoted by the MMS to settle in "heathen" parts and spread the gospel by example rather than precept. Ten of the twenty-three came for the Moravian station at Fairfield; only one couple had returned by 1849.

Early BMS Jamaican missionaries had a less satisfactory welcome in Fernando Po. There was an appeal to the Society in 1846 from the Norman family in Spanish Town to bring back one of their relations and seven of his colleagues. They enclosed letters that they had received from the Jamaican missionary party in Africa stating that they wanted to come home because European missionaries in Fernando Po were treating them with contempt, worse than they regarded the Africans themselves. There were, furthermore, no arrangements for sending their children for education, either in Jamaica or in the UK.[22] This was an interesting case of the "missionary culture" being applied to the situation of Jamaican missionaries in Africa. They expected respect from their European colleagues and, from the BMS, support for educational opportunities for their children similar to that offered to European missionaries. More successful was Thomas Keith, an African-born ex-slave, who after emancipation worked his way back to his native land to teach his own people; he reported that a further mission from Jamaica would be appropriate and profitable. This led to the arrival of John Clarke who brought with him a group from Jericho where he was serving as a BMS missionary. The Jamaican members included Richard Merrick and his son with Alexander Fuller from Spanish Town with two of his sons.[23]

The Baptist Calabar College was started with the preparation of Jamaican missionaries for West Africa as one of its main purposes. From the pioneer start missionary service became a regular feature of the

Jamaican BMS community. It was yet another opportunity for self-expression for young men emerging from the chapels and day schools, seeking fields of service appropriate to their undoubted ability. They were obviously a source of pride to their families and to their chapel communities. It is not hard to understand why the Fernando Po group and their relatives in Spanish Town saw no reason for them to be regarded as inferior to European missionaries.

Similar problems of status arose in Jamaica between, in the first place, European and "native" schoolmasters; in due course the emergence of "native" missionaries brought similar contention. European missionaries reported from time to time that their members preferred a European pastor or schoolmaster. This was probably true in the urban areas or where, for instance, a black teacher was introduced into a station from another part of the island. In their own communities coloured and black teachers were more often regarded as successful runners in the social mobility stakes and won respect accordingly.

The Jamaican coloured pastors who were gradually accepted into all the missions were exceptionally hard-working in virtually all cases, and could empathise with the vicissitudes of their own people as the socio-economic decline took its toll on the living standards of the labouring population. Robert Johnson, John Vaz, Alexander Foote, Alexander Lindo and, in due course, Richard Parnther, Thomas Geddes and William Clarke Murray won allegiance in their own right as Jamaican religious leaders in various parts of the island. It is worth noting, for instance, that at the time of the rising in Morant Bay every missionary pastor of whichever mission was a Jamaican, apart from one who was away at the time; they remained at their posts and did, with one notable exception, all that they could to mitigate the crisis and its sequel.

There were some notable cases of the Jamaican membership of chapels maintaining a disagreement with missionary "authorities" for long periods of time. Perhaps the most publicised was the dispute over the BMS chapel in Spanish Town in the 1840s.[24] The most striking aspect of the affair was the strong position taken up by the officeholders and the members of the chapel. They not only expressed their opinions unanimously, but also addressed themselves directly to the BMS in London. Their claims to authority in the matters arising in the dispute, as well as their sympathies, can be simply demonstrated in the postscripts to two of their letters to the BMS at the beginning of the contention. In

Jamaican Initiatives in Missionary Christianity

the first communication they were objecting to a rumoured decision to send Dowson, the junior missionary, away:

> Information having reached us of the meeting of the Sub-committee [of the BMS missionaries in Jamaica], stating that they advice the Revd. T. Dowson to leave Spanish Town so that they might be piece in the church but we deem it as necessary to detain him as our Paster instead of J.M. Phillippo. We sorry to say that we cannot oblige the sub-committee for it is the Wishes of Both the Trustees and deacons and also three parts of the congregation of Spanish Town that he shall go no further and where he is.[25]

Another Dowson supporter among the trustees acknowledged the BMS' right to direct the movements of its own missionaries, but pointed out that the Society could not cut off the station itself "as the chapel and mission house is our own property and we can do what we like with it. The Church is quite strong to maintain her rights" the writer concluded.[26] In this instance the members were regarded as "The Church" rather than the European missionaries. The mode of maintaining their rights demonstrated the strong desire of the officeholders and members for recognition as decision makers in their own chapel. They were extremely indignant about BMS' responses to their early representations and resented patronage from any English ecclesiastical source.

In bitter recriminations against Phillippo for what the trustees regarded as his sharp practices they obliquely reminded the Society of their common British citizenship. "We been long ruling under Moral dispirit," they asserted, "and we will suffer no more high Priest to rule over us, for we thank God that we have a Gracious Queen who will defend all her subjects from the hands of a Spiritual Tyrant."[27] Whether the Baptists of Spanish Town really thought that they had an effective royal champion in the Defender of the Faith and head of the Anglican Church in England is open to doubt, but it makes good protest reading. That the trustees were resisting English patronage is clear. "The committee at home must think us to be fools and void of knowledge; but no our Eyes are fully opened to the World to know good from bad", they assured their fellow British citizens in London. The trustees in their claim to control their own chapel in Spanish Town borrowed some of the European missionaries' own habitual defences through the Queen, "at home".

The letters were highly critical of Phillippo's record in Spanish Town, and of the whole BMS mission in Jamaica, in collecting money for their own support. Even the missionary contribution in setting up free villages was criticised; Phillippo was castigated for buying land and selling it "for treble the value" to establish Sligoville – "in fact doing more than the planters", wrote his accusers. The whole BMS mission was criticised. "The greater part of the mission is dealing in traffic rather than Engaging to the Spread of the Gospel throughout the Land", claimed the Spanish Town trustees. In conclusion, they reported that, with the deacons and members, they had taken the key of the chapel, handed the case over to the High Court of Chancery and now declined to accept the Rev J. Phillippo any longer as their minister.[28] The trustees did not propose discussion and compromise; they had not been consulted in the first place.

The end of the dispute, when the High Court finally ruled in favour of Phillippo, was a predictable secession from his congregation. Dowson's supporters built an independent Baptist chapel in Spanish Town which he served, and they attended, until his death fifteen years later.

The whole affair was fraught with bitterness and attitudes of a sociopolitical cast despite the religious rhetoric which abounded. Phillippo must sometimes have regretted the success of his schools in Spanish Town; they presumably had contributed to the self-confidence and the articulate protest which his officeholders and members were able to sustain on their own behalf. Any shortcomings in spelling and syntax did nothing to mask the sentiments of the writers, and were in any case shared by several of the British missionaries themselves.

Assertions of their rights were by no means confined to the better educated, socially aspiring chapel members in the large towns. Participation in the choice, or sometimes the rejection, of a pastor was in effect quite common. The members of the LMS station at Mount Zion took this initiative twice and, after considerable procedural delays by the European missionaries, won their choice on both occasions. The first contest took place in the last half of 1843. The LMS proposed to transfer their missionary, Edward Holland, and leave the settlement with only their European schoolmaster, William Hillyer. The members, if they were to lose anyone, overwhelmingly preferred to keep the ordained pastor. The issue became embittered because of the very laboured interventions of the LMS missionaries from neighbouring stations, who felt it their duty to uphold the LMS decision. Barnett, a deacon, was spokesman for the

Jamaican Initiatives in Missionary Christianity

Mount Zion members and tried to discuss the matter with visiting LMS missionaries at the 1 August emancipation commemoration celebrations. Finding them intractable he "made use of very improper language" and, with his followers, left the gathering "in a tumultuous manner, exclaiming against the proceedings and threatening to write to the Society". The visiting missionaries appear to have been equally impetuous, for they expelled Barnett from chapel membership on the spot.

The matter was now a confrontation. It seems remarkable that a remote settlement of ex-slave smallholders had the skills and shrewdness to conduct an effective dispute against European missionaries far better educated and with an inborn certainty of their own superiority and authority in the context of this decision. The Mount Zion members got up a petition to the LMS drawn up by the native Baptist schoolmaster (said to be a former white overseer sacked for drunkenness). They declared that they would leave the LMS chapel unless the ordained missionary remained with them.[29]

The next stage of the confrontation was equally contentious. The LMS missionaries set up a subcommittee to investigate the validity of the members' petition; three of their members travelled to Mount Zion to examine each signatory individually. Since there were 170 signatures it is not surprising that in the event the people lost patience with the proceeding; when their leader, Barnett, was called they entered the meeting with him en masse. Everyone understood that they were petitioning for the retention of their ordained pastor Holland, and that they would indeed transfer to the native Baptists if he were to be removed. To emphasise their sense of grievance they declared that they would send in a bill to the Society "for every bit of money we ever subscribe to this station". Like other protesters in the chapels they asserted their relationship with the missionary body concerned. "We aint going to be humbugged by the Society", they declared. One suggested that they transfer forthwith to the native Baptists; he tellingly pointed out that then, "you will have a minister that will never be removed except by death".[30] Half the membership did in fact transfer before the year was out.

Hillyer, the schoolmaster in the case, had actually been in the station longer than Holland, the ordained missionary, and was able to explain the details of the people's grievance. They had originally offered £313 to the Society to bring out an LMS missionary for their new settlement. They subsequently agreed to transfer these funds to rent a house for a schoolmaster. They then raised a further £105 to get their first missionary but he was soon transferred. Now that they had lost one missionary and were threatened with the loss of a second they were incensed. Furthermore, Hillyer described the provocation maintained by the native Baptists of the settlement. "Them will laugh at we," Barnett had told Hillyer, "because the Society make fool of we. They give we two ministers, now take them both away." This is what you can expect if you insist on having white ministers from abroad, maintained the native Baptists of the village.[31]

In November the people of Mount Zion sent a second petition in favour of keeping their missionary. To save on postage they did not include their second page of signatures, but the first page contained 83 men's signatures and 69 women's (including 33 pointedly designated "Mrs"). It is a fair inference that, despite the heavy departure to the native Baptists, there remained even more LMS supporters who wished to enter the fray than in the case of the first petition. The petitioners again warned that the station would break up if they did not get their way, and produced a fine clarion call for the people of a remote settlement in the early postemancipation years. "We are also of the opinion", they declared, "that no good can be done by any man who opposes the will of the people."[32] It would appear that they had once again recruited the literary gifts of the native Baptist ex-overseer. What nevertheless seems very clear is that despite the disbelief of their missionaries, the LMS members of Mount Zion well understood and approved of the petition that they were presenting on their own behalf.

The upshot of the dispute was that, despite a contrary view that Holland would always be under the thumb of Barnett at Mount Zion, the members got their way. The clinching argument was simply that they would abandon the LMS station if they did not. Several of the missionaries remained affronted by this defeat; others, however, approved of the people's claim and the outcome of a very real confrontation involving a question of European versus native rights in a Jamaican settlement in the Clarendon hills.[33] As a footnote to the Mount Zion affair it can be noted that the members retained their right to a say in the appointment of their pastor. When Holland left them in 1852 the deacons (one with his written signature and three with an X) applied for the return of Hillyer, the schoolmaster, on the condition that he now be ordained for the office. In this case they would do all in their power to support him.³⁴ Their proposal was accepted and acted upon.

Other LMS stations adopted this method of obtaining ordained pastors for their communities. With the agreement, and sometimes the nomination, of the members several European schoolmasters were ordained for service in new stations requiring an ordained minister. Examples were John Gibson and James Milne who were ordained on taking up their ministry at Davyton in 1844 and First Hill in 1847 respectively. Every LMS missionary in Jamaica attended Gibson's ordination and the people of Davyton turned out in force; in a severe year of drought they contributed fowls, "bread kind" and corns for the celebration.³⁵ Six years later they nominated their own schoolmaster, Lillie, to be ordained as successor to Gibson, to ensure that they kept a minister at their station.³⁶

The Davyton members took their initiative still further when Lillie was transferred in 1853, in successfully requesting the ordination of a Jamaican coloured schoolmaster/catechist to serve them. Alexander Lindo was at the time in demand at two stations. He had served the LMS for twelve hard years as a schoolmaster/catechist, first in Four Paths and then in Morant Bay; it was in the latter that he also received a unanimous vote for his appointment as missionary to be ordained at the station. In the event Davyton was the successful bidder. Lindo's ordination there was a well attended celebration. Eight LMS missionaries, one Methodist and one Presbyterian, were present in addition to the population of Davyton. As the first native missionary for the LMS Lindo declared "a new era in the Jamaica mission" and hoped that he was only a pioneer as a fellow labourer with European missionaries.³⁷ In effect the Davyton Chapel chose their own minister three times running selecting a Jamaican on the third occasion.

Sometimes members could be as strong in condemnation of their missionaries as they were in approving or nominating them. Two interesting cases arose in Morant Bay. Benjamin Franklin was a successful missionary in the station from 1838. He had also married a Jamaican woman. Seven years after his arrival the wife was seduced by Deacon Cummings, an Englishman who had been living in the mission house for the past few years. "As a missionary and a Christian" Franklin felt compelled to drive both his wife and the deacon from his house. He consoled himself with the reflection, "Thank God *my character* is without a stain."³⁸ Regrettably for the missionary the Morant Bay members did not see the affair in the same light. They ranked compassion and forgiveness above rectitude, and regarded Franklin as merciless in not pardoning his wife and having her back. Throughout 1846 they withheld the money collected in chapel and in classes, sending it instead to Mrs. Franklin who was staying in Kingston. Franklin was finally forced to resign and leave the island when the chapel members brought his wife back to Morant Bay, in a hired coach and pair, to stay with two of their number in a house only fifty yards from the LMS chapel.[39] This was a confrontation about Christian values between a missionary and his members which lasted for over a year and a half. The definitive action of the members led to a victory of compassionate pardon over unyielding morality. It is a matter for surmise whether the members would have been so strong in her defence had the lady not been a Jamaican.

Franklin's successor, Josiah Andrews, drew the opposition of the members at Morant Bay for entirely different reasons. He made the mistake of going to live with an overseer and, according to the members, "minds not his own work". The members at Prospect appealed directly to the LMS to remove him because they claimed that he had not been seen in the chapel for four months, had never visited the school and would not recognise a member of his flock if he met him in the road. Other missionaries, they emphasised, visit the people in their homes and "never go to sport and gallop horse with overseers as Andrews is doing". The petitioners for his removal warned that many members had already left the chapel. They also took the occasion to resent complaints that their contributions were small. "If it is so," they argued in their petition, "it has a right to be small after there is no one left in the place to help those few that remaineth, so there can nothing good be made." Finally they challenged the LMS, if they did not believe their Jamaican members, to send an officer from London to find out the truth at first hand.[40] It was not only the missionaries themselves who invited headquarters to send observers to the scene.

Andrews did not depart as quickly as his predecessor. After a visit home to Britain, he returned for another year to Morant Bay, where he in fact distinguished himself by strongly supporting the nomination of the schoolmaster/catechist, Lindo, to be his successor; it was he who reported that the congregation, who had known Lindo for eight years, had voted unanimously in his favour. Andrews's Jamaican career was in fact terminated in Mandeville, again after representations from the people. He was

Jamaican Initiatives in Missionary Christianity

again neglecting pastoral visiting and was reported to be very oppressive in the raising of money.[41] He was away on yet another home leave at the time. In the way of most chapel groups fighting their own case the petitioners declared that they would leave the church if he was allowed to return; this time he stayed at home. It was the juggling to fill his vacancy which brought Lindo first to Davyton and then to Porus.

By the 1850s many lay members of the chapels obviously felt that they could, and should, influence missionary appointments even if they could not make their chapels self-supporting. Newly literate generations used their communication skills to address unknown mission secretaries in London in uncompromising terms, and good Jamaican protest language, including biblical phraseology. If this did not secure the end in view they could, and did, simply transfer themselves elsewhere. The lay influence in the chapels grew. As a positive element it made the chapel serve the perceived interests and the preferences of each particular community. When they were resisted the withholding of funds and the threat of transfer to other religious groups were effective ways of at least checking unwanted developments by European missionaries.

The emergence of Jamaican missionaries to serve in the clerical role varied between the denominational missions. The need for reinforcement, increasingly unlikely to come from Britain, forced European missionaries to consider seriously their attitudes towards the development of a native ministry. The home societies, always short of funds for their expanding activities at this period, were more inclined to press for a native ministry than were many of their missionaries in the field. The BMS and the LMS missionaries in Jamaica were the first to see that they could not extend their work unless they had many more pastors to open new stations. The older Methodist missionaries in particular continued longest in their opinions that, firstly, their members preferred European ministers and, secondly, Jamaicans did not yet have the education and the training for the office.

From the perspective of an increasing number of Jamaicans it must have been hard to see how their teacher/catechists, who preached every Sunday after teaching the day school pupils all week, were not ready to become missionaries themselves. It was mainly from this group that the first ministerial candidates emerged. Others were from coloured families who had been free long enough to attend to the education of their sons in the private schools set up for this social group. Some of these early

Jamaican missionaries adopted European attitudes, and emphasised their British citizenship, even more strongly than did the European missionaries themselves. All of them, however, were strongly committed to the development of their own people and sympathised fully when their members were unable to finance the chapels. There must have been an empathy between them which differed from the compassion of even the most concerned European missionary.

The Jamaican missionaries demonstrated between them most of the attitudes of the upwardly mobile postemancipation population; they also developed a resistance to colonial attitudes in their European colleagues. The WMMS mission in particular continued to promote the idea that West Indians would make good missionaries for West Africa. Their main argument was that they would be better suited to tropical conditions than Europeans. In the general enthusiasm for converting their African brothers people did not observe that tropical conditions also existed in the West Indies, or that West Indians might be better conditioned culturally than Europeans to work with their own people. In the circumstances there was some ambivalence about ordaining Jamaicans. The first four Methodist Jamaican missionaries were all in the first place destined for Africa while they prepared for ordination. In the event they all remained in Jamaica where they were sorely needed by the mid 1840s when they were ready for appointment.

The attitudes of the Jamaican missionaries to their work, despite their adoption of European missionary culture, seemed substantially different from those of their European colleagues. They were Jamaicans with nowhere else to go; they were committed to both the conversion and to the social betterment of their own people in the taxing years after emancipation. Some of them thought that they were not only equal in value to their European colleagues, but even that they were more so. Alexander Foote's declaration at the time of his ordination indicated a kind of brotherhood in his commitment to the members of the Bath Chapel where he began his ministry: "I am resolved to be a man of one Science – Salvation", he stated, "of one business – Saving myself and those who hear me."[42] He linked his own prospect of salvation with that of his hearers. It is similarly noticeable that all the Jamaican missionaries wrote in their letters about "my people", instead of "the people" more commonly reported by the European missionaries. The feeling of identification with their followers was marked even though their

Jamaican Initiatives in Missionary Christianity

religious practices and, more particularly, their moral strictures were European in tone.

It is not surprising to find that the Jamaican missionaries tended to proselytise more energetically than their colleagues in the postemancipation years. They made considerable inroads into parts of the island not yet reached by their missions. Examples are John Vaz who expanded the Methodist holding in Manchester;[43] Robert Johnson and Henry Carter, who were mainly active in upper St Ann;[44] Alexander Foote in Manchioneal after Bath. These missionaries also tended to try unconventional methods of reaching those who increasingly dropped out of the chapels. All of them adopted extensive outdoor preaching to large crowds who did not have to be concerned with their appearance before they could attend. Alexander Lindo held very well attended pre-dawn prayer meetings with workers in the Porus district and organised his chapel members for a systematic domestic visiting programme to the unconverted of the neighbourhood. Archibald Monteith's pastoral visiting in Westmoreland and St Elizabeth continued over decades until his death; Moravian missionaries considered his work indispensable to their mission although they never made him one of themselves.[45]

The relationships between any of the missionaries, let alone between European and Jamaican, were limited by the fact that they were widely dispersed. They saw far more of their teacher/catechists, deacons and leaders than they did of each other. They called upon the help of their neighbours, including those of different missions, when travelling, for special addresses to the auxiliary missionary societies and even for preaching. Annual meetings for the pastorate of any mission became increasingly irregular and poorly attended. Even Methodist missionaries, who needed to attend their annual District Meetings for the three-yearly postings to new circuits, excused themselves on the grounds of expense or because they could not afford for other reasons to be away from their circuits for some three weeks on each occasion. In these circumstances the relationships between European and Jamaican missionaries seldom arose as an issue until the question of differentiation of payment and treatment was raised by some of the societies in London.

On occasion, however, the Jamaican missionaries chose to distinguish themselves as such. Alexander Foote was notable in emphasising both their identity and their importance to the mission. Explaining the decline in membership in Manchioneal in 1846 he included "the lack of a local agency" as one of the factors. The postemancipation generations, he pointed out, were looking to become more comfortable in life; when depressed wages limited their capacity to pay chapel dues they stayed away because they could not "answer the call of the Society, as some of them term it". Foote obviously thought this was a false sense of values which could be corrected by more ministers and instruction through "a native agency".[46]

In Manchester, John Vaz, who called himself "a poor son of Jamaica", held the same view that the problem for effective proselytism was the lack of missionaries to reach the growing number of dispersed settlers. He described them as "decent people of colour and many emancipated blacks", who had no access to missionary Christianity or schooling in the interior parts of Manchester, St Elizabeth and Trelawny.[47] He knew that he was not dealing with irreligious fellow citizens; their failure to encounter missionary Christianity was, in his view, a deprivation, not a resistance on their part. Vaz himself was a great believer in house to house preaching; "private conference is indispensably necessary", he claimed. In Kendall he preached in a booth used for dances to the "wretched men and women" who formed an impromptu congregation. "I tried to deliver my Soul", he wrote. The Jamaican missionaries seemed still to concentrate on conversion when their European colleagues felt constrained rather to service those already converted in their established stations.

It was Foote again who mobilised his fellow Jamaican Methodist missionaries to add their names to a memorandum which the European missionaries were submitting concerning signs of opposition to Wesleyanism, in England. The Jamaican memorialists somewhat virtuously asserted that despite "the Demon of confusion, misrule and dissension among . . . some of the Christian gentlemen of England, we, the Wesleyans of Jamaica, are resolved by the Grace of God to hold the Wesleyan faith in the unity of Spirit, in the bond of peace, and in the righteousness of live [sic]".[48] This was clearly a case of Jamaican insistence that they too were concerned in the state of Wesleyanism in England. Was it also a case of "colonialism in reverse"?

Lindo of the LMS raised an issue which would lead to dissension in any of the missions. Their home societies had always been more enthusiastic for a native ministry than European missionaries in the field who advised delay. The pressure from London was clearly for financial

Jamaican Initiatives in Missionary Christianity

reasons. Led by the BMS and the LMS the home committees wanted the Jamaican missions to become independent of their financial help as soon as possible. In this context they advocated native agencies which should be less expensive than European missionaries.

Lindo pointed out that there were strict limitations to this economy if it was to be acceptable in Jamaica. Three years after his ordination he was finding it impossible for his family and himself to live on £120 a year; he stressed that the only savings that the LMS should make on native ministers were the costs of a transatlantic passage and a tropical outfit as required by the European missionaries. The living costs thereafter were identical.[49] Seven years later Lindo was still complaining that his salary, after twenty-five years of service to the LMS, as teacher/catechist and missionary, was less than that of a European who had arrived yesterday. He stated where the Society had gone wrong in the matter. "I know that the smallness of my pay", he asserted, "is founded on the *incorrect data* [sic] that a native, though he is sufficiently respectable to worthily represent your great and noble Society can be less expensively – rather *less decently* (maintained) than a European."[50] It is noteworthy that Lindo wished to emulate the respectability and decency of his European colleagues; it was a matter of status and respect for a minister whatever his origin. His consistent objection to the differentiation of salary was undoubtedly shared, and could explain why the LMS had to retire from the island when they could no longer afford to send out Europeans; they had not attracted a sufficient Jamaican ministry to take over.

The BMS missionaries in Jamaica, who had optimistically declared themselves financially independent of the parent society in 1842, realised that, however difficult their financial position became, they would not retain their Jamaican colleagues on a differential salary. They rather hoped that the Calabar graduates would in the end take over their own Jamaican church and would then settle their own financial dispositions. Unfortunately the small numbers of students gave no prospect of such an outcome in the near future.

The WMMS mission probably produced the most clearly formulated arguments for and against the unequal payment of native and European missionaries. The native pastors, and the lay leaders, were very ready to watch Jamaican interests at any time. Some of the elderly Wesleyan European pastors provoked lively response when they approved of their Society's proposal for differential salaries in 1863. On the other hand

63

Edmondson, now over forty years a missionary in the West Indies, begged his committee not to press their proposal. It was altogether too late in the day; it had never before been suggested that the earliest native Methodist missionaries, the ex-slave Edward Fraser, Robert Johnson, or Herbert Carter, should be treated differently from their European colleagues. Now their successors "have lived with the expectation they would never be reduced on account of the colour of their skin". Edmondson could predict that their resentment at the change would cause them to transfer to the Established Church, or go into business, or, perhaps worst of all, remain in the mission with a constantly expressed grievance about their treatment as inferiors in their own country. Finally, with long experience of independent protests by the Kingston stewards, he anticipated that the lay members would register their disapproval of the proposed measure by holding back their dues.[51]

Edmondson thought that the best policy was to follow the example of the other missions in setting up a training institution to increase the number of Jamaican ministers. He felt that Jamaican Methodists still preferred European preachers; on the other hand, they bitterly resented any slight to a native missionary. "If you attempt to oppress the native, because he is a native", he warned, "you will bring a nest of hornets about you immediately."[52]

The chairman knew that he could not rely on all his colleagues to support him in the matter, the veteran, John Corlett, for example wrote a *"Strictly Confidential"* letter to the WMMS proposing a systematic differentiation in the Jamaica mission. Native ministers should be appointed to the stations and pay themselves from the collections and quarterly paid class dues; while salaried European missionaries should be superintendents visiting each station once or twice in each quarter.[53] The indications are that Edmondson was at least able to keep this inflammatory proposal from the eyes of the Jamaican missionaries and their champions in the lay membership.

While the European missionaries referred to their Jamaican counterparts as "native" ministers, delicately avoiding any reference to the colour of their skins, the Jamaican missionaries themselves saw the matter as essentially one of colour. Fraser, seeking an English education for the orphans of his deceased Jamaican colleague, Carter, went to considerable care to describe Carter's status in Jamaica as a coloured man. He was a "high caste" man, the son of coloured parents, his father in

Jamaican Initiatives in Missionary Christianity

public service employment. Fraser obviously felt the need to point out that there were "high caste" coloured people in Jamaica; it was not enough that Carter had achieved his place as a missionary in his own right regardless of his colour or his family's social status. Perhaps Fraser saw it as a good opportunity to instruct the Society in the facts of Jamaican life. He certainly ended his letter with the hope that native ministers' children were eligible for education in English Methodist schools, as their European counterparts were.[54]

Alexander Foote entered into direct and critical contention with the WMMS. In 1863 he withdrew from the Methodist Preachers Annuitant Society because he suspected that it was no longer open to native missionaries.[55] He had already earlier in the year addressed the Society on their ignorance of Jamaica and their stupidity in comparing it with the "two tedious examples" of Australia and South Africa. More than that inappropriate juxtaposition he had deplored their implied attitude that a poverty-stricken church like the Jamaican one should be a despised church. "One is tempted to think", Foote wrote, "that even in the church of our Lord Jesus Christ poverty is becoming a crime." He concluded by suggesting that missionary officials in London should come to Jamaica "to enlarge their discoveries."[56]

In the event the district meeting of October 1864, accepted equal cuts in missionary salaries for Europeans and Jamaicans alike. Those in attendance stated that if the WMMS wanted any other measure they would have to impose it themselves.[57] Whether or not the Jamaican Methodist missionaries found out what had been proposed in 1864 for their differential remuneration by the WMMS is not certain. Notwithstanding, they sent by far the most telling letters to the Society impressing upon them their responsibility to serve the Jamaican mission in that year of distress. Foote wrote an able eight-page account of the financial position of the island to show that there was no foreseeable way of meeting chapel debts, or other deficiencies in the district accounts, unless the WMMS was prepared to help. Effectively the survival of the mission, and of European Methodism in Jamaica, was in the Society's hands.[58] Thomas Geddes was similarly clear on WMMS's responsibilities. He asked how the Society was able to reconcile their withdrawal of support with their former acceptance of all the free labour and contributions which had been provided by the poor people of his country.[59]

W. Clarke Murray applied himself at length to the related issues of WMMS's refusal of an English education for the Carter orphans and the need for Foote to bring back his sons from Taunton School in England for lack of funds to keep them there. He declared that he himself could not cope with an inherited debt for Bath Chapel, and to appeal to the members for help would be to taunt them with their poverty. Murray's address to the Society was in portentous terms which could hardly have been bettered by those Victorian gentlemen themselves. "I cannot believe", he wrote, "that my acceptance of any measure of finance which will destroy my reputation, sap the foundation of my social and domestic happiness, and incapacitate me for the discharge of Divinely-enjoined parental duty will be an offering acceptable to God, and ought I to be required to present it?", he asked rhetorically.[60] Murray was very much on his dignity in claiming his due. The order in which he placed his disadvantages with an inadequate salary is most interesting. It was a moot point whether his large family, or indeed that of most of his European colleagues, could be regarded as divinely enjoined; but in any case his domestic needs come second to the potential destruction of his reputation in his statement of hardships brought about by poor remuneration. Reputation as an abstract quality has been well discussed as a feature of the Caribbean male psyche;[61] it appears as a basic motivation for the leadership in the chapels, more particularly for Jamaican missionaries themselves.

In 1864 the defence of the Jamaica Methodist mission was far stronger by the Jamaican missionaries than by their European colleagues. They were defending their own church against what they regarded as a misinformed, if not ignorant committee in London, in both Jamaican and English senses. The WMMS must have realised that they were dealing with no inarticulate native ministry who had accepted an inferior status to the European missionaries. The statement of Jamaica's economic plight by Foote and Geddes, for example, was far more detailed, wide-ranging and clear than any presentation by the Europeans. The survival of the Jamaica mission was emphatically their personal cause. A year later they would again be sending their own characteristic reports on the Morant Bay revolt and its sequel. Although still in a minority in the mission they had developed a distinctive outlook and a strong commitment to the interests of their own countrymen.

Not all Jamaican missionaries stayed the course in the dissenting ministry, any more than did the lay chapel constituency. Of the earliest resignations both Vaz and Johnson withdrew because they got into financial difficulties; suggestions by some European colleagues that dishonest dealings were involved were certainly not substantiated. Johnson went on to become the editor of a revived *Watchman*, was elected as a member of the House of Assembly and migrated to the USA in 1866 when there were hints that he might have been involved in planning the Morant Bay riot.

Alexander Foote's resignation in 1866, to become a minister in the Established Church, was also ostensibly for financial reasons, although he was at the same time being criticised for writings in favour of the blacks in the American Civil War. Foote was the most bitter of the Jamaican brethren about what he regarded as colour discrimination in the missions. His target remained the Society in London. He felt strongly that they should have supported the men, rather than measures of economy, to ensure the survival of a Jamaican Methodist Church. If they were unwilling to offer patient support they should now hand over the mission to the native ministry, for better or for worse. "Hand over the once magnificent mission to an economical native Ministry", he recommended. His accusation of colour prejudice was bitter. "The darker the complexion the more economical is, I am told, the idea in England – hand it over to a dark and economical – necessarily economical because naturally dark, native ministry which has never laboured in or visited England. So let the mission go – on to the dogs – on to the dark . . ."[62] Foote at least had identified colour prejudice as the cause of neglect by the WMMS.

By the time of the advent of Crown Colony government to Jamaica in 1866 the British nonconformist missions had fostered, and accommodated, an independent nonconformist awareness amongst the struggling but respectable communities which supported them in Jamaica. Both the lay membership and the Jamaican missionaries supported the missionary culture with its European social and moral values in what they regarded as their own churches. European missionaries and their offspring who remained in Jamaica joined a discernable emerging middle class which allowed them in succeeding generations to find new sources of "reputation" in what was now their own land. After the disestablishment of the Church of England in 1870, by a British Colonial Office initiative, the Protestant churches in Jamaica and the rising Catholic Church offered a new opportunity for Jamaicans in their secondary schools, and a combined arena for the expression of social aspirations in new capacities, including teaching in the ministry and in the schools of the various churches.

The original role of the dissenting missions in conversion and proselytism was to pass to others, in a different mould, who related better with participatory, pentecostal or revivalist activities of Afro-Jamaican Christianity. The European missionary role in the Christianisation of Jamaica was arguably as much a social as a religious development. It provided an arena for aspiring ex-slaves eventually to create their own middle class on a Euro-Christian model.

CHAPTER 4

Jamaican Christian Groups

I belong to a body who simply desire to be called Christians.
"Minister" Arthur Beckwith to Royal Commission, 1866

By the 1860s Christian practice was more broadly led by Jamaican than by European models. The Protestant missions were contracting rather than expanding; the native Baptists and other independents filled the gaps not reached by the Europeans; they had also challenged new European missionaries in the field. Because they had no coordinating machinery throughout the island it is impossible to quantify their membership. It was, however, large enough, and articulate enough, by the 1860s to alarm the colonial authorities, custodes and magistrates as well as the ministers and pastors of the European churches. The two main sources of information are missionary writings and the evidence given to the Royal Commission of 1866 which enquired into the circumstances of the disturbances following the Morant Bay riot and its subsequent suppression. Both sources were highly suspicious of the intentions of the numerous small native Baptist communities and contemptuously critical of what they regarded as an ignorant, illiterate and misguided population. It is from this, at best equally ignorant and at worst hostile, evidence that the truth of Jamaican Christianity in the decades after emancipation has to be derived.

In the first place the majority of Jamaicans of the time simply called themselves Baptists. The term "native Baptist" was adopted by those who wanted to distinguish between local Baptists and the membership of the BMS chapels; this was not helped by the fact that "Baptists" who could reach a BMS preaching station on the Sabbath would probably combine this with more active participation in their community Baptist group at other times. It would appear that Jamaican Baptists themselves were by no means as concerned with the distinction as their European observers were. An exchange between John McLaren, one of the leaders at the Fonthill meeting house, and the Commissioners in 1866 illustrates the viewpoint of both:

- Q. What denomination do you belong to?
- A. Baptist.
- Q. What society of Baptists, the native Baptists?
- A. John the Baptist.
- Q. Do you belong to the Native Baptist Society or the one in England?
- A. No understand.
- Q. Is your society a Buckra society or a nigger society?
- A. Nigger society.[1]

The Commissioners no doubt regarded the episode as further evidence of the ignorance of the Jamaican peasantry. They were in fact themselves wrong in referring to the "Native Baptist Society". There was no such organisation. John McLaren was no fool. He was the father of James McLaren who wrote the communication from the Stony Gut protesters to the Governor on 10 October 1865, and was executed under martial law for complicity in the rising. His father was clear that his son could read and write, but could not preach. The Fonthill community had their discriminations too. The Royal Commissioners no doubt had even more difficulty in understanding "Minister" Beckwith who claimed he had a chapel in St David and was a travelling preacher in the Blue Mountain Valley; he declared that he belonged to "a body who simply desire to be called Christians".2

There seems little evidence that denominationalism was an important factor in Jamaican Christianity outside the European churches. The common ground was that independent Christian groups were led by Jamaicans and designed by Jamaicans to meet their preferences in forms of worship and to confront the worldly problems of living in "freedom" in an increasingly impoverished society.

Jamaican Christian Groups

The extent and the range of the Jamaican Christian groups appears to have been much greater than the European missionary reports indicated. When appealing for extra resources for their own activities they tended to suggest that "the enemy" was paganism and barbarism whereas, in a variety of ways, it was a growing Jamaican Christianity that was the rival to the missionary culture. The missionaries were oddly reticent about their breakaway groups such as the Pennockites and the independent Baptist chapel under Dowson in Spanish Town which were undeniably Christian in their own mould.[3]

Until the mid 1840s the native Baptist groups were strongest in districts which the missions had failed to reach. This was best revealed by the LMS when they arrived in 1835. They were particularly concerned to set up stations where the older missions were not established. Not only did they find themselves contending with many native Baptist groups but also they found positive resistance to European missionaries in favour of their own leadership, their black preachers and "daddies".

Woolridge, the senior member of the first six LMS missionaries to arrive, reported his observations with a prejudice which he probably acquired from other missionaries in Kingston. In a list of the city's chapels he included "Lyle's and Killick's", classified as Baptist with those of *Mr* Gardner and *Mr* Tinson of the BMS. Liele had in fact died in 1826, but Woolridge declared that "Lyle and Killick are black men, ignorant, disreputable and unrecognised", except presumably by the 900 members of their chapels whom Woolridge also reported; his instinctive hostility to the native church apparently prevented him from even getting his facts right before condemning it. He also discovered that many communities in the country districts had formed native Baptist groups "for want of other"; one group near Spanish Town had recently baptised eighty candidates, for example. After three months in Jamaica he declared that the native groups "bring the profession of religion into contempt".[4]

In one respect Woolridge was right. The Jamaican groups were strongest in the country, and often opposed to any European missionary expansion in their districts. An enthusiastic Methodist missionary in Port Morant reported the prevalence of "native agents who are endeavouring to injure and destroy Methodism in this circuit".[5] At Bath a young missionary identified one of the motivations of the native groups; he reported the alternative that the people had in the native Baptist and "Methodist breakaway groups", mainly started by expelled members "careless and impatient of reproof". They felt safe in these societies, the missionary explained, so they left the mission chapel and were immediately received into a native church.[6] Robert Johnson, the Jamaican Methodist missionary struggling to service a circuit a hundred miles in circumference from Mandeville, warned that "the ignorant native Baptists are very numerous and possess great influence" in the extensive sugar estates of Vere.[7]

The experienced Methodist Chairman, Edmondson, recognised new developments in the native Baptist churches which perhaps he respected rather more than most of his colleagues. Reporting on a tour of his district in 1845, he conceded the native Baptist groups equal place with the Established Church and the BMS chapels as Christian rivals to Methodism. Furthermore he did not represent their preachers as the dusty itinerants of the past. "A number of men who could not be employed by us have purchased black silk gowns, etc. and begin to form societies under the denomination of *native* Baptists and *native* Wesleyans," he explained. Furthermore they were drawing off WMMS members with critical statements such as that the Jamaican chapels, built and paid for by Jamaican Methodist members, were now claimed for "Mr Edmondson's father", meaning presumably the WMMS in London.[8] The reason that Edmondson thought that "they could not be employed by us" was probably that the leaders were still largely illiterate, as well as that many had already been expelled on moral grounds. What he revealed was a group of independent Jamaican preachers seeking to demonstrate an equivalent validity with European missionaries, both symbolically in their dress and also in the claim that they had led the people to Christianity in the first place and would remain with them thereafter. It was no doubt groups of this order which now set about building their own chapels or more modest meeting houses, and taking a pride in their own initiatives.

The consistent opposition of native Baptist groups to the LMS occurred in Clarendon, Manchester and a small part of St Ann at Dry Harbour when they sought to establish stations where other European missions were sparse. They were opposed because native Baptist leaders had become a considerable force and were unwilling to give up their local authority. Furthermore the LMS missionaries were no more ready to adopt their leaders than was the Methodist Chairman. William Alloway developing a station in the Dry Harbour area declared it to be a well-populated district "destitute of religion". Yet when a deputation of native Baptist leaders offered their services, bringing their groups with them, he declined on the grounds that the LMS accepted only individual volunteers; he suggested further that he should teach the leaders to read.[9] There were no more offers of cooperation in this northern LMS station; as it was always in difficulties it can only be assumed that the people decided to remain with their own. They were certainly not destitute of religion.

At Porus the LMS missionary was bounded by five flourishing black Baptist groups which he found "a barrier to the spread of true religion".[10] Conversely, eight months later the Porus congregation was much reduced because the vigilant Baptist leaders were impressing upon their followers that the LMS themselves were not offering true religion; this was an opportune conclusion from the fact that the mission was evangelical, but undenominational. The condemnation of each others' Christian religion was mutual. The Porus missionary found the native Christianity to be the work of "the subtle adversary of the church, subservient to the souls of men". The black leaders effectively questioned the credentials of a European mission. *"Massa leader* move me attention to it", explained one of the many who withdrew from the now suspect LMS chapel.[11]

William Barrett at Four Paths confirmed the strong organisation of the native Baptist groups in the area when he was invited by a Special Magistrate to visit the Parnassus Estate. He found it to be the "stronghold of this system in Clarendon" and "a literal den of leaders". One was Shaw, the estate blacksmith, who preached to large crowds and whose "almost unbounded influence" extended as far as thirty miles into the interior of the parish. Another power at Parnassus was Allen, an expelled BMS leader; he was literate and had assumed the role of a minister with a church admitting, as Barrett maintained, members "living in open whoredom".[12] LMS attempts to oppose the black preachers on the Parnassus Estate simply failed; the European missionaries conceded the territory and withdrew.

The power of independent black Christian leaders on the estates was remarked on by missionaries of all denominations. The Presbyterian, Hope Waddell in St James, found them wholly authoritarian, exercising the powers of an African potentate.[13] They were often the headmen or, like Blacksmith Shaw, the skilled workers on the estates. They were not pressing an unwelcome form of worship upon their followers. On the contrary they were organising in independent communities practices of

Afro-Jamaican Christianity which maintained traditional values and, precisely because they were not a coordinated denomination, could adapt to local challenges rapidly. The most prevalent features of the native Christian sects were the importance and symbolism of baptism by immersion, conducted in mass meetings by the river or the seaside; the importance of dreams and visions to a mainly illiterate membership; the encouragement of dance and song as a spontaneous sign of repentance or of thanksgiving; the retention of Myal medicine and other practices in a Christian context.

Above all, these relatively small religious groups, formed within an estate or a settlement of smallholders, dealt with many common needs on a community basis. As the socioeconomic circumstances of the people deteriorated after the mid 1840s the native Baptist and other independent groups clearly adopted a social role in attacking their own local problems. The members of the missionary chapels who threatened to transfer their allegiance to the native Baptists did so not only to avoid missionary dues and chapel moral strictures, but also to join groups contending specifically with their own urgent problems. A case in point was the tendency of native Baptist groups to handle their own legal difficulties rather than to take them to the magistrates' courts where "planter justice" alone prevailed. Many native Baptist sects established their own courts on the pattern of those started long ago by the American Baptist, Moses Baker. As literate members became more common in the native churches the communication skills of those who had learnt to read and write were available for petitioning and protesting. These were the initiatives which alarmed Governor Eyre in 1865.

In the 1840s the one great advantage that the mission stations could offer over the native preachers was instruction in their day and Sabbath schools. The early emancipation thirst for literacy was largely met in these schools; those who attended the day schools also learnt to write, to calculate and to regurgitate formidable amounts of "useful knowledge". As most missionaries realised, their great appeal at this stage was that they could teach people to read. They strengthened this advantage by condemning illiteracy as a major failing in the native preachers; without the ability to read they could never propagate a biblical Christianity. Loyal native Baptist followers counter-attacked with assertions that true Christianity was received through the Spirit not through the Word. "Dem no go by de Book, but by dem Hearts", declared Moses of Mandeville, an illiterate preacher who claimed to be John the Baptist himself. As a clinching argument he concluded that "Massa Jesus himself no go by de book."[14] "Daddy" Pennock in Blue Mountain Valley maintained that he learnt much more from God's Spirit revealed in dreams, visions and voices than he ever found in the Bible. Indeed he went further to report that if he fell asleep with a Bible or prayer book on his chest when he had had a vision, on waking he found the pages blank.[15] The vision took precedence over the Word.

The CMS missionary, Sedden, had an unusually perceptive communication, for a European missionary, with an American black preacher, again near Mandeville. The preacher's resistance to biblical over spiritual Christianity was that many people had learnt to read the Bible but they did not believe it; "'em get no good from it because 'em neber believe it", he contended.[16] What the preacher may have meant was that the newly literate did not understand the Bible; he may also have meant that the Bible was not in fact their prime target in learning to read. The frequent references by native Baptists to the limitations of biblical Christianity in the early years after emancipation were probably a defensive attitude at the point where literacy was still widely sought after by ex-slaves. A Bible in fact soon became the centrepiece of the chapels and the humble meeting places that the native Baptists built themselves in due course. Time no doubt also remedied the problem of illiteracy. There seems good reason to assume that where a Sabbath school was within reach the Baptists attended with others who did not belong to the chapels precisely to acquire such instruction as they all aspired to. It is unlikely too that the only native Baptist day school was to be found in Mount Zion.[17] Literate native Baptists emerged among those associated with the Morant Bay riot, for instance.[18]

The representations of the other missions against the BMS missionaries in Jamaica in the 1840s no doubt contained the concerns of all of them about the nature of Jamaican defined Baptist Christianity.[19] The independent values and practices of black Baptists emerged clearly from the critical expositions, though the charge that the BMS was promoting them can be discounted. Most of the "charges" were substantially true of the native Baptists and were indeed their attraction for their independent followers. To understand the account from the point of view of the black Baptists themselves, it is of course necessary to ignore the missionary outrage at what they described, and instead to recognise the Jamaican popular purpose in their forms of worship and their codes of morality. The basic criticism was that these Baptists were unscriptural, had no books and learnt Christian hymns by heart. Since rote learning was also much practised in the mission day schools it was odd to object to illiterates more understandably teaching themselves the same way. The enduring ability of Jamaicans to quote the scriptures at length has been demonstrated in churches, chapels, fields and squares over the years. It has been the response to limited educational opportunity as well as to the methods used in the schools.

Discipline was said by the critics to be so lax in the Baptist groups that it could be regarded as connivance at crime. This criticism does not coincide with the known powers of the black leaders over their flocks. The difference lay in what they regarded as punishable offences. The missionary critics complained that fighting, drinking and fornication were not regarded as sins by the Baptists. Yet they themselves presented the case of a distressed Baptist member who had been "put back" for six months for not cleaning the path to the schoolroom. The distress of the offending Baptist member was as great as that of any expelled missionary follower. He worried, it was reported, that "if death should meet him during that time he did not know what to do, for the leaders say, *if they put the people back, God puts them back, and if they take them on, God takes them on*".[19] This "putting back" would have been a ministerial function in a missionary chapel. It is clear that the black leaders did in fact exercise strong disciplinary powers but were probably more concerned about offences against the common good rather than matters of personal morality. It can be inferred that they exacted penalties for such offences as theft and praedial larceny from each other, physical harm and failure to work on agreed services. These were evils traditionally dealt with by the obeahman. It is perhaps not surprising that in some villages the obeahman was reported as participating in raising funds for the support of the black Baptist preachers.

Other particular practices deplored by the missionaries in their complaints against the BMS following were long standing in native Baptist groups. These were the "setting off" or "bowing down" to initiate new candidates into kneeling for prayer, regarding John the Baptist as more important in Christianity than Jesus Christ, the holding of Friday fasts and, above all, the convince or the getting of the spirit. The missionaries were constantly contending with the prevailing belief that baptism constituted a final commitment to Christianity. Common statements were "when we get baptize it all done" or the use of the phrase "he has got through". One extreme resister of missionary approaches found even baptism redundant. She contended that she had cried at her birth "and at that moment I cried for my sins", so, she concluded, "God heard me and pardoned me then; so I am in no danger of going to hell."[20] The woman's statement not only reveals her anxiety to resist the British missionary; it also shows that he must have presented the threat of hellfire as the cornerstone of the Christian religion. There is evidence that this missionary emphasis alone deterred many from adopting "the white man's Christianity". A local version embraced more of the current spiritual and temporal needs of ex-slaves who had already experienced hell on earth.

The leadership of the native churches was largely determined by whoever in a local community could attract a following. The number continued to augment as former deacons and leaders of the missionary chapels, often in the neglected remote districts, declared their independence from their European mission and took their flocks with them. Black deacons and leaders virtually monitored all the religious and moral affairs of their flocks with sometimes only bimonthly, or even just occasional evening visits from the station missionary. It was almost a reversal of roles from the slavery days. The native deacon or leader increasingly became the established religious force in his community; the European missionary, however unwillingly, became the itinerant preacher. This was not only in remote stations. The BMS missionary Gardner, of East Queen Street Chapel in Kingston, had 3,000 members scattered over twenty square miles; as a consequence four of his deacons left the chapel taking their classes with them and offered baptism, preaching and communion to anyone who would pay them the ticket money instead of the BMS. One interesting sequel to this independent initiative was that it attracted several black members of the LMS chapel in Kingston to transfer because they would be relieved of the need to attend classes to qualify as converts in that very exacting mission.[21] Several of the older BMS missionaries concluded that only one in ten members of *all churches* were in fact converted, by which they meant that they were faithful followers of the missionary culture in all respects, without diversions. Woolridge of the LMS, was of the opinion that the black Baptists were by contrast recruiting "hundreds a year".[22]

The choice between missionary membership and membership of an independent native group was by no means only fortuitous. There is plenty of evidence of doctrinal discussion amongst simple people. The missionaries could have learnt much about explaining their message from one woman at Mount Regale who was asked if she thought she could be "saved by dreams or Convinces" alone. Her reply suggests a very real discussion at village level about the essentials of the Christian religion. "How can I", she answered "when that Bible Book in your hand says sinner heart so wicked that it requires God's holy light to make it wise, and his grace to pluck up the roots of sin." This might well have been the missionary version of what she was supposed to have said; what follows, however, sounds more authentic as a typical Jamaican elaboration of an important point. She continued, "Suppose when me go to the river to wash clothes must me not soap them and rub them? If me fall asleep on the pass and dream they are all washed, will me find them so when me open me eye? No, Minister, only Massa Jesus Christ blood can convert we heart or save we poor soul." This exposition was accompanied with exclamations of "True, sister, true" by others present.[23] The whole reply seems calculated to reach the woman's fellow villagers in a settlement where the native Baptists were in the majority, and where there must have been much argument between the two congregations. Although the black pastor provided the resort for a growing number he too must have encountered a multiplicity of doctrinal points gleaned from various sources – the Bible, the preachers, black and white, Myal traditions – all related to the taxing life experience of the postemancipation generations. Ongoing discussion of Christian doctrine must have been a feature of life in Mount Regale, and most other settlements.

One of the many native Baptists in the Mandeville area "proved" that Jesus Christ was second to John the Baptist by asserting that Jesus was "in the wilderness" before he came into this world. Another dealt with the vexed problem of the significance of the crucifixion of Jesus by making it a matter of divine discipline. "Him farder tell him him must come from dis world, but him no bin want to come because him tink we would kill him", explained one debater, "den him Farder said, if him no come him will punish him – den him 'bliged to come." The missionary reporter cited this as an example of the ignorance of the people.[24] Another interpretation is that it shows the earnest concern of simple men and women to bring their religion within their own understanding and experience. The second theological theory quoted may well be debatable, as no doubt was intended, but it hardly seems an entirely erroneous explanation of Christ's words on the cross. The pity of it was that the missionaries could see these discussions only as debased Christianity, if not rank heathenism.

The Jamaican love of disputatious discussion was scarcely allowed for in the chapel congregations. In particular the missionaries failed to recognise the general difficulty over the concepts of personal sin, the meaning of repentance and the atonement, simply because they endlessly reiterated this doctrine rather than attempting to discuss it. The generations born after slavery were particularly alienated by an interpretation of the Christian religion which both neglected their current distressing problems and also limited their opportunity to relate themselves actively to religious teaching.

A good demonstration of the difficulties of candidates in reconciling Christian doctrine with their own experience was provided by Sam Oughton, the BMS missionary, who kept a record book of his examination of candidates for baptism; he also carefully noted his reasons for either accepting or rejecting each. It is revealing to consider some of his reasons given for rejecting candidates. Here are six examples of observations on those "set aside":

- Does not see his need for Christ, says water will wash away his sins at one time and then his heart was clear from sin.
- Never met with one so ignorant who had sat so long beneath the sound of the Gospel. Never thought of the immortality of the soul.
- Ignorant of the way of salvation.
- Dark concerning resurrection and other matters.
- Trusting in his own merits for salvation.
- Does not see the necessity of the atonement.

At least two candidates asserted that God would show mercy at their day of judgement and explained how this could be ensured by Afro-Jamaican practices:

- Says her soul will rise on the third day – that the class sit up all the first night to pray that *God may have mercy and receive the soul into Heaven.*

– Says that the soul will rise on the third day and that if a brother should die in his class he would meet with the rest and pray that the Lord Jesus would have mercy on the poor soul.[25]

The concept of a merciful God to whom intercession can be made at the time of death related with the custom of laying evil spirits in the Nine Night activities. As an alternative to a devout and moral life of Christian worship and repentance it was clearly unacceptable to Sam Oughton and his colleagues; they had by now presented the ever present dangers of hellfire loud and long for many years. After rejection from missionary communities for holding another view of the same God it is little wonder that so many transferred their allegiance to the black preachers. They increasingly articulated their concern for a Jamaican Christianity to recognise the preoccupations of the mass of the people and to deal with their growing predicaments in both religious and secular life. The native Baptist communities saw their religion as a daily resource in the community rather than simply the means of personal salvation.

The fact that the native Baptists were black and native were attributes exploited by their preachers. Those followers who also attended missionary chapel services were assured that they would not understand the white preachers, but that the "daddies" would explain it all to them afterwards.[26] A newly arrived LMS missionary to remote Mount Regale in 1842 described the hold of the black Baptists there. "Crimes were committed", he claimed, "for which even Tetzel would be ashamed to sell an Indulgence."[27] This vivid European Reformation reference may have been well appreciated in LMS headquarters in London; it would have been right outside the experience of any Mount Regale resident, however well primed with European "useful knowledge". A year later the black Baptists were taunting the people for building a home and buying land for a European minister who "when he has obtained all he can get, he will run away from you".[28] The attempt later in the same year to substitute a schoolmaster for the missionary has already been discussed.[29] Although the grievance was one for the LMS membership only it was fuelled by the black Baptists of the community, who ensured that it became a dispute between native and foreign, black and white. They encouraged a large transfer of LMS members to themselves on the argument that they would thus ensure that "you will have a minister that will never be removed except by death".[30] This was open confrontation in a small settlement.

Although in the event the missionary remained he continued to do so amidst an overwhelming majority of black Baptists, who in this settlement had further strengthened their position by maintaining their own school and asserting the superiority of the native preacher. This was no longer a case of an illiterate, uninformed leadership. Another assertion of a preference for a black preacher occurred in Porus in 1846. When the BMS missionary returned to England that year the members declared themselves opposed to "another buckra minister". A black minister appointed temporarily was dismissed for immorality a year later. A hundred of the Porus members still opposed the appointment of a European missionary and withdrew to form their own Baptist group, "in our very midst", as the LMS missionary reported.[31]

In short, independent native chapels were being established in towns other than Kingston and in the ever increasing number of small settlements and villages set up by freeholders and those who increasingly rented small plots of land from the estates. Distance from missionary encounters remained one factor, but there was also confrontation when people chose a native Christian group as a deliberate alternative to mission chapel membership. Furthermore they were building their own chapels and meeting houses, maintaining their own black preachers and seeking their own standards often equivalent to those of the missionary culture. In Morant Bay for instance land was bought at Church Corner and a chapel built as early as 1838. Two years later the black preacher requested a horse and chaise from his people and was charging them 3/6d for a ticket and 1/8d a week "as the mite to be thrown up". The LMS missionary reporting these developments acknowledged that "the daddy" appeared to be an intelligent man who had been in "Parson Kellick's" congregation in Kingston.[32]

In general the European missionaries recognised that the black preachers were gaining ground but nevertheless persisted in denying their Christian character. They tended to relate the growth of the native Baptist influence with the general apathy to religion which they also constantly deplored. Wilkinson in Kingston was really alarmed by the spread of black chapels. As he saw it, "the people's views of religion seem generally to include only dreams, visions and fastings, and 'drawing to table' as they call partaking of the Lord's Supper". He felt that he was contending not only against idolatry, but also against "a false and fatal security".[33] Most of the people appeared for their part to have lacked any meaningful communication with European missionaries. They found them unsympathetic to Jamaican mores. Even those who sought membership of the chapels grew weary of the ever lengthening time of preparation and delays in getting ministerial approval for their acceptance. Perhaps most of all the majority of Jamaicans craved active participation in their worship based upon traditional Afro-Jamaican practices.

Mistrust seems to have grown steadily between the missionaries and those who adopted independent religious groups. Congregations led by blacks, especially as they established themselves with their own meeting houses and even schools, increasingly criticised white preachers who expected to be maintained by the local population, but who were not committed to remain with them. In short missionaries came to be classified with the colonial official "birds of passage" and the absentee landlords. This was an exaggerated attitude. The majority of missionaries remained in the country for many years, often decades, while their families were born and grew up in their stations; many put down their roots in Jamaica and had no intention of returning to Britain. Their shortcoming was not a failure of commitment but a failure to understand the values of those who remained outside the missionary culture and increasingly had vigorous religious aspirations of their own. The missionaries consistently failed to recognise the Christian core of the alternative black religious groups. They could not accept a community based morality derived from long established resistance to social evils, in place of absolute doctrinal standards of personal morality. Mutual understanding was not possible without communication. As the mass of the people sensed a lack of missionary sympathy in their worsening circumstances the gulf between European Christianity and the Afro-Jamaican forms widened progressively.

The missionaries and their "respectable" followers failed to recognise, let alone exploit, Afro-Jamaican Christianity. Waddell, who expelled members even for using Myal medical practices, was not only critical of, but active against, a Myal revival in the western parishes in 1842. The ban had been lifted after emancipation and it can be assumed that the revival was mainly celebratory. Waddell described the activities as "the strongest combination of Christianity and heathenism ever seen". He also noted that most of the participants were in fact members of one of the principal missionary churches, doubtless the BMS. His response to groups arriving in his station to "cleanse" homes of evil spirits was to instruct his followers to keep them out. He himself engaged physically in breaking up a session by pushing through the circle of dancers and occupying the central space. They were, he reported, "sailing around and wheeling in the centre with outspread arms and wild looks and postures" accompanied by singing in a low monotonous tone. Although Waddell could not understand the chants he was made to know that he had climbed on a chair right over "the hidden poison". After considerable objection to being regarded as mad the group finally retreated to a nearby house "where they began to sing something like a hymn, and closed their ceremony, it was said, with prayers".[34] Waddell reported them to be "baffled" and "disconcerted"; it would be interesting to learn their understanding of his own action in the matter. The episode demonstrated the irreconcilable differences between the objectives of a Presbyterian missionary and the estate people's notion of infusing Christian hymns and prayers into demonstrative religious traditions of their own. There is little doubt that the celebrators regarded themselves as Baptists and Christians.

Another group in 1842 were taken before the magistrates for trying to hold their meetings in a BMS chapel. They appeared with their heads bound, swaying throughout the proceedings and declaring "We no' mad. It is the Lord Jesus Christ. We de dig out all dem badness."[35] On this occasion it was the officers of the court who were "amazed" and no doubt, like Waddell, quite unable to accept any Christian connection with the activities they were witnessing.

The arrival of 8,000 African immigrants in the years between 1845 and 1865 injected fresh African spirit into the island. Their two main areas of settlement were St Thomas-in-the-East and Westmoreland. In early years, when African immigrants still had hopes of returning to Sierra Leone where many had been recruited, they and their religious practices remained aloof from their Jamaican neighbours. When it became apparent that there were to be no passages home, they started to integrate more fully into their local communities. They seem at first, however, to have been more concerned to retain their African roots than to make new Christian connections.

The beliefs and practices of these post-slavery African immigrants have been well discussed by Monica Schuler and Mervyn Alleyne.[36] In the context of the Christianisation of Jamaica they seem particularly important for introducing new African ritual for Afro-Jamaican Christians to add to an already well developed synthesis. It was reported that African obeahmen were more highly regarded than their creole counterparts. Kumina is a St Thomas survival which may have originated in slavery or was introduced by Congolese immigrants arriving via St Helena in the mid nineteenth century. It seems certain however, that the later arrivals reinforced Kumina practices, even if they did not introduce them.

The Yoruba immigrants in Westmoreland were mainly "recruited" in Sierra Leone where they had probably already encountered missionary Christianity through the West African activities of the WMMS and the CMS. They seemed readier to accept Creole lifestyles and were influenced by the Baptists. They adopted the system of deacons and meetings in their Yoruba community. The Yoruba *etu* was retained as a social dance, at weddings for instance, rather than as a ritual as in the case of Kumina.

The new Africans as they accepted their future in Jamaica did not ignore the Christian churches. Some sought literacy as much as the creole working people, and attended the missionary chapels for the Sunday school classes. Where they proceeded to membership the Baptists were the most attractive, particularly for the baptism by immersion which recalled African river gods and the power of water spirits. In St Thomas-in-the-East where there was only one BMS missionary stationed the Africans joined the numerous native Baptist groups and no doubt added greatly to their religious activities.

Convince was the most significant survival of practicing Myalism. It was the experience of visions and dreams which induced the spirit and for the native Baptists, gave evidence of conversion. Convince, according to Alleyne, was introduced into the Baptist groups by Myalists before emancipation. The Congo Africans in St Thomas "re-Africanised" Myalism by injecting their Kumina practices. The importance of Convince and the spirits was thus fortified for the development of Afro-Jamaican Christianity. In due course the emergence of such groups as Pocomania, Revival, Zion and Holiness strengthened the link between the African and the Christian manifestations of spiritual religion. The essential elements in each reconcile for their followers African beliefs, in convince, the dominance of the spirits and the cleansing power of water, with Christian affirmation of the rites of baptism and the prospect of salvation in the life to come. They maintain in Christian worship maximum participation for each member and a hierarchy of officeholders giving each distinctive and active roles in the expression of their faith.[37] This was in contrast to the members' place in European based chapels and churches where their participation was limited, formalised and directed, and their full membership often delayed for years. Above all, as worshippers in Afro-Jamaican forms of Christianity they were frequently visited by visions and possessed by spirits, ancestral and Christian-referred, which offered them ecstatic expression of their emotions; in the chapels by contrast they were constantly castigated as sinners with little encouragement to express even their penitence demonstratively. The Revival of 1860-61 revealed what had been lacking in the appeal of the missionary culture to the majority of Jamaican people.

Nineteenth century missionaries in a colonial setting were unlikely to recognise, let alone sympathise with, the underlying expectations for religious life of the mass of the people who did not, or more often could not, adopt the lifestyle of European "respectability", the hallmark of chapel membership. The decline of the missionary influence after the first years of emancipation was not only due to their own lack of resources to expand their proselytising, nor even the alien character of so many of their social and religious values. The situation was that a poor and struggling population found a more acceptable religious expression in a synthesis of traditional Afro-Jamaican beliefs grafted upon Christian teaching and applied, under Jamaican leadership, to the circumstances of Jamaican communities. The strength of the alternative Christianity tends to be lost in the missionary and official sources which periodically report its existence without understanding and usually without respect, let alone sympathy.

Not only did Jamaican religious forms offer participation in worship and ecstatic experiences, they also offered opportunities for initiative and self-expression to people who had little other chance of asserting their identity. As the euphoria of emancipation was replaced by the actualities of hard living in a declining economy, religion was needed to fortify a native resourcefulness rather than to promote an alien form of respectability. Where the missions had presented a Christian lifestyle to grateful ex-slaves, their children and grandchildren increasingly sought Jamaican Christian alternatives to deal with a society which had not fulfilled the first expectations of freedom for social mobility.

CHAPTER 5

The Great Revival

Oh happy day, Oh happy day,
When Jesus takes my sins away.
Sung on the roads during the Revival

The Great Revival which began in the last months of 1860 demonstrated all the Christian influences at work in Jamaica. Whether or not the initiators of the Jamaican Revival were aware of similar movements in Britain and the United States is not clear; it is, however, very clear that the Jamaican Revival was started and orchestrated by the Jamaican populace, largely the young people. They drew on all their religious experiences to express their desire to be born again and to adopt a dedicated religious way of life. The chapels were used, but the movement extended to the highways and byways in activities soon unacceptable to European missionaries. The Revival has been called a triumph of Myalism. It was certainly a revelation of the strength of Afro-Jamaican Christianity.

The movement began in the highlands of Westmoreland in the last months of 1860. Revival activity then spread along the north and south coasts, reaching the eastern parishes in the early months of 1861. By May the missionaries were already regarding the upsurge of religious fervour as a dying movement. Tyson in Brown's Town reported in April that the chapels were still overflowing, but the "intense excitement" had died down; he had had no prostrations in his chapel for some six weeks past.[1]

The Great Revival

Thomas Raspass in Savanna-la-Mar was reporting "hundreds of marriages" and a vastly increased membership, but doubted his ability to sustain the effect in his chapel activities.[2]

While the fervour was dying down in the west of the island it was just reaching the eastern parishes. The Jamaican Methodist missionary, Foote, reported that the Revival had reached Port Antonio in February and Manchioneal, his station, in April 1861. It was still proceeding there in July. "It pleased God to visit us with his Holy Spirit; cries and protestations since then have been the order of the day, and sometimes nearly all night," he wrote. Like all the missionaries, Foote's first reaction was to encourage the crowds who filled his chapel for hours on end; he observed them offering up spontaneous cries of repentance and extempore appeals for forgiveness of their sins, accompanied by much demonstration of their feelings with groaning, beating their breasts and prostrating themselves with grief at their spiritual condition. The missionaries did their best to inject their own teaching, exhortations and prayer into the proceedings, and certainly succeeded in obtaining unprecedented numbers of new candidates for membership of their chapels. At the height of his early optimism Foote found that "the conversions are clear, scriptural and delightsome".[3]

The Revival expanded, however, not simply as a chapel invasion. The promoters took to the highways and byways of the countryside and increasingly adopted Afro-Jamaican expressions of worship which greatly upset the originally enthusiastic missionaries. "The folly of superstition" was soon, for example, observed by Foote in Manchioneal and its outstations; furthermore he thought this was innocent as compared with "the sickening nonsense, and worse than nonsense, of so-called Revivals in some other parts of Jamaica".[4]

Foote's report at the later stages of the Revival describes the original exaltation set against the growing doubts of the European missionaries. In the early phases while the revivalists took to the chapels, and conducted prolonged and demonstrative penitence there, the missionaries strove to play a part; they were encouraged because many sought chapel membership by joining classes; many were married and the local vices of drinking and gambling were much reduced. While overwhelmed and by no means in total control of the chapel based Revival, the missionary pastors regarded it as an authentic change of heart which they should attempt to service with utmost effort. On the other hand, they were increasingly aware of another Revival conducted outside their chapels which adopted native Baptist and Myal activities. This was what they condemned as superstition and folly. By doing so they disassociated themselves from the Revival experience of almost certainly the majority of the people involved.

It is important to consider what the population had in mind and how they assessed the effects of their own Revival movement. There is no doubt that it was initiated by the people, that they adopted their own procedures and that insofar as they included the European missionaries in the activities, they determined their role. The pastors did not themselves arrange for the chapels to be inundated day and night by penitents expressing themselves in extempore ways; nor were they able to contain most of the demonstrative activity. The revivalists used the chapels and the ministers' services at their own discretion, not the missionaries'.

The activities of the Revival outside the chapels were totally unacceptable to European pastors who learnt little, if anything, from the Afro-Jamaican Christianity there displayed. In the end the native version preponderated; there is little doubt that membership of native churches and the following of black preachers were more promoted by the movement than the revival of the missions. The documentation of a remarkable event remains, however, the European missionary reports. Reading between the lines, and avoiding their prejudices, it is possible to consider what happened in the months of the Revival and in the years immediately following.

In its first manifestation the Revival appeared to the missionaries literally as a godsend which might be their rescue from years of decline in their chapel membership. The fact that crowds took over the chapel premises for hours and days on end to maintain extended expressions of repentance and hope for salvation was the very response, perhaps less vigorously expressed, that the missionaries had so long sought. Despite the wailing, groans and often prostration that signalised the repentance, the missionary response was to participate insofar as they were able to. Over months they preached and exhorted tirelessly at all their chapels and outstations; they enrolled hundreds of candidates and conducted many marriages.

The Revival proceedings in the chapels, however, were not dependent upon, let alone led by, the ministers. Two of the most vivid accounts of missionary experience during the Revival came from the LMS pastors, William Alloway near Mandeville and Duncan Fletcher in Chapelton. Alloway realised early that he was not to be the source of inspiration for the movement in his district. He was certainly a spectator on his first encounter with it. Summoned by a deacon to the Moravian schoolhouse at Broadleaf he witnessed a mixed crowd of Moravians and his own people "engaged in praying and exhorting in a loud voice". No one was presiding over the activities and they took no notice of Alloway. At first he felt that the people were doing wrong, but then he changed his mind. He noted the sins that they were so anxiously repenting:

> Some were kneeling, weeping and praying: confessing their sins to God, naming them – their neglect of Divine ordinances, unbelief, hardness of heart, sins of commission, and their secret sins – This they did audibly; sometimes not only specifying and deploring their crimes, but also praying for their companions in guilt, by name.

Others were consoling the distressed penitents and exhorting a growing crowd of spectators to join in, "some of them the vilest of men", remarked Alloway. He added, however, "I saw no mockers – not one." The missionary managed to inject a hymn and a half-hour address into the proceedings, and thought this would bring the exercise to an end. But, some having thanked him politely for his contribution, "they all resumed their engagements". Alloway now realised that his visit had lasted five hours, and there was no sign of an end to the penitential activities. On the following Sunday he was able only to deliver his sermon in the LMS chapel after "the stricken" had been removed until the service was over.[5] He was at best an auxiliary, not the agent, of revival in the Mandeville district.

Duncan Fletcher in Chapelton was better able to exploit the movement. He considered that he achieved more in three months of the Revival than he had done in his previous four years at the station. There was a week in November 1860 when the LMS chapel was thronged night and day almost constantly "with men, women and children weeping and wailing aloud for their sins. A scene so solemn and overwhelming, I thought could not be witnessed prior to the judgement day", wrote Fletcher. He joined forces with the Rector to form a Church Fellowship class of some 400 candidates. His comment that "they comprised some of the most intelligent and many of the most ignorant of our community", demonstrated the wide appeal of the Revival. It was by no means a popular movement in the sense that it was confined to the marginal population of the hard times. The missionaries found their own "respectable" members present with hundreds of others who at most had previously only been on the fringes of Sunday chapel attenders. The "two Jamaicas" on this occasion demonstrated their thirst for a Christian religion on their own terms. As Fletcher put it, it was "union and peace among all classes".[6]

Perhaps because their members were involved and because the first effect of the Revival was a large new recruitment of candidates for their chapels the missionaries at first plunged themselves into the action rather uncritically. Their preaching was extended to the open air; hundreds of marriages were performed; new Christian associations and benevolent societies were formed. The pastors were gratified by the closing of rum shops and gambling dens and the absence in 1860 of the usual Christmas festivity with dancing and drumming. Demonstrations of religious fervour applied to repentance were not unwelcome to the missionaries. The Moravian Buchner was pleased to come upon a communicant "lying on a mat on the floor writhing under the agonies of an awakened conscience". The penitent's sins in this case consisted of rum drinking and, interestingly, failure to pay church dues. "We tell minister", he confessed, "we have no money to pay the church when we have plenty at home." Buchner also reported that many in his station were casting out articles thought to be associated with sin, such as furniture, clothing, jewellery, and even their shorn hair.[7] This was presumably in response to regular ministerial criticism of ostentation and display in those members of the chapels who could afford it.

The veteran Methodist missionary, John Corlett in Montego Bay, was an enthusiast for the Revival and was perhaps the earliest to engage in extra-chapel support for it. He described a day in December 1860 when he took to the road. From the first crowd that waylaid him on the way he baptised twenty on the spot, received seven others on trial and, having providentially carried his marriage register with him, was even able to marry a couple. He stopped at several of his leaders' houses to meet large gatherings at each. "At every mile," he reported, "I was hindered by penitent enquirers and I found one prostrate on the side of the road as if dead." Finally he returned to a huge interdenominational gathering at the BMS Chapel in Montego Bay, which went on all night.[8]

The Great Revival

Few missionaries in the early months of the Revival seem to have anticipated the popular interventions into the movement outside their chapels. Holdsworth at Grateful Hill observed that the two native Baptist preachers and one native Methodist were leading the activities in his circuit.[9] Hillyer at Mount Zion reported in January 1861 that not only was his chapel filled to overflowing but also that many revivalists were travelling and waylaying others in the road to give them the spirit. He was disturbed by "a large amount of superstition, terror and blasphemy", which included women representing themselves as the Virgin Mary or calling themselves the Lord Jesus Christ.[10] It may be assumed that the Mount Zion native Baptists controlled Revival activities in that settlement.

Increasingly the Revival spread outside the chapels, along the roadways and into people's homes. Here elements other than demonstrative penitence and prostration entered in. Obeahmen participated in the Revival on their own terms; only at Sawyers did the local "King of the Obeahmen" join the prayer station for the Revival.[11] The strong resurgence of Obeahism in St Thomas-in-the-East, no doubt fortified by the African immigrant element, caused Foote to remark that the whole movement in Manchioneal had become in his experience a mixture of ecstatic joy, on the one hand, and extravagant superstition and folly, on the other.[12] At Yallahs another Methodist missionary also reported that Obeahmen had intruded to spread confusion and disorder among his new young converts; in this attempt "to kick the Revival" one had even died in his frenzy.[13]

At Guys Hill "fanatics" took over the Methodist Chapel while the missionary was away in Kingston for the annual district meeting. To his horror Obeah practices had been introduced there. He observed what he described as dancing in circles, signs of possession, eating earth, biting the ground, crawling on all fours, making animal noises and, to add insult to injury, he himself was told that he was standing on the wrong spot for the time of day, as bad spirits then prevailed. At his outstation at Mount Roper the same missionary expelled *"prophets, prophetesses, visionaries, trumpeters, Dummies"*. Some were taking a sacrament using cologne and water instead of wine.[14] Six months later he found that several of "those extravagant young people" were now pregnant. They included a "Queen" who had revelations from heaven and saw hell without a covering, where she also saw the missionary himself. He was astounded at her influence in the district; "she had only to say do this, and a host was ready to do it", he marvelled.[15]

Had the Guys Hill missionary paid more attention to the regular practices of the native religious groups abounding in his area he might have been less outraged, and would certainly have discerned customary religious activities not only associated with the Revival. The visions and possession by the spirits were prevalent in the Myal related aspects of the Jamaican Baptists. The young Jamaican Methodist missionary, Thomas Geddes, now beginning his pastoral career at Port Royal, was far more perceptive; he recognised the "visual element" in the Revival experience of his members. He explained that the people when prostrated could actually *see* their sins and Satan, and then finally they experienced a vision of Jesus.[16] The cologne used for a Lord's Supper may simply have been more readily obtainable than wine; the independent Baptists had celebrated the ordinance for years and in this case appear to have made a convenient substitution. The "prophets and prophetesses" expelled at Mount Roper no doubt resorted to one of the local native churches, if they were not in double membership already. As another missionary at Linstead later remarked, what he regarded as the excesses of the Revival were mainly performed by the "Baptists".[17]

Probably the most balanced summing up of the effects of the Revival came in a resolution moved by Duncan Fletcher and adopted by a meeting of the LMS in February 1861. On the one hand, they gratefully acknowledged "tokens of genuine conversion to God in the remarkable Revival of religion so extensively enjoyed in this island". On the other hand, they could not but "deplore the superstition which has developed itself in connection with the gracious movement among the less enlightened portions of the community".[18]

In the year following the strongest manifestations of the Revival, missionaries had mixed reactions to its real effect. They were disappointed to find that they soon lost many of the young "converts" who had become candidates during the period of excitement; they predictably had to expel many others for committing "the sin of the country". Critics deplored the fact that much work and planting of food crops had been neglected while the revivalists wandered through the countryside in search of converts and attended lengthy Revival sessions. On the other hand there was a moderate lasting increase in chapel membership, largely by those who formerly had only attended the preaching sessions. It was also considered that those who sustained their conversion and remained faithful were now far more spiritual and devout than in former years, though this was mainly only among "the old Christians".

In short, the missionaries came to recognise the limitations of the movement for lasting recruitment to their chapels without drawing any consolation from the strength of the movement outside. By relegating the strongest manifestations to "the less enlightened portions of the community", they again closed themselves off from an increasingly impoverished population, and so put a seal on their prospects of any conversion to European, nonconformist, "respectable" Christianity for the majority of the population. So the original British missionary purpose, to raise up a hard-working, respectful, God-fearing peasantry on a British contemporary model, was at last shown by the events of the Revival to be an aspiration of the past.

By 1862 there was little further reference to the Revival in missionary correspondence. They had reverted to their money problems and their disappointment with the home societies for wanting them to become Jamaican churches independent of their parent bodies. Summarising in a letter of 1864, one missionary judged that not only had most of the Revival converts now disappeared again from the chapels, but that they had also become embittered and were a bad influence in their communities. In fact the price rises created by the effects of the American Civil War on imports now exacerbated abiding poverty and increased the resentment at the missionary clergy's constant appeal for funds. Several pastors realised that they were better known as money collectors than as spiritual guides.

Because the missionary version of the Revival hardly persisted in their chapels there is little written evidence of the lasting effects of the whole widespread movement. There can be little doubt that the majority of the revivalists were motivated by the native Baptist and Myal forms of the movement. It can also be assumed that these groups grew rapidly in the 1860s. Thus they ensured that Afro-Jamaican Christianity was confirmed as the preference of an absolute majority of the population. This might be judged to be the fundamental achievement of the Revival which was overwhelmingly an assertion of Jamaican preferences in the practice of Christian religion.

Just because the revivalist groups sprang from Baptist, and or Myal, influences with no islandwide organisation, the expression of their religious outpourings was spontaneous and often contradictory. Drink was abhorred by some; libations of rum were required by others. Sexual freedom developed with some manifestations; it was condemned by others. Some native Baptist groups maintained the taboos set by their originators, the black American preachers, some eighty years earlier; they rejected sexual relationships outside marriage and the use of alcohol.[19] Such limitations were not, however, accepted by other Baptists or by those who were still mainly Myal practitioners. The activities of most of the revivalists no doubt derived from a wide range of intermediate beliefs along the poles of the Afro-Jamaican religious experience in local groups.

The Revival promoted, and was probably activated by, the central activities of Afro-Jamaican Christianity. It involved maximum spontaneous worship by its followers; this included the getting of the spirit, prostration, rhythmic movement and sound and little concern for the European set service. Where a shepherd or prophet held forth his utterance was punctuated by extempore supporting prayer or exclamations. Baptism by immersion had become central to most Jamaican religion. Funerals, wakes and the Nine Night persisted as the means of settling the spirits of the departed, and in most cases dealing with antagonistic spirits which threatened in general. This was, and is, what is meant by spiritual in the revivalist sense.

Monica Schuler suggests that the Jamaican Revival was finally taken over by the Myalists. It would probably be more accurate to say that it was vigorously adopted by the native Baptists and other black independent groups, in association with those Myal practices which they already maintained in different degrees according to each group's particular disposition. In the emotional fervour, Myal related activities no doubt were more observable than the less demonstrative practices of the same groups. It is highly probable that native Baptist churches gained a considerable membership during the Revival. Several Methodist missionaries, including the Jamaican Clark Murray in Lucea, reported a big swing to "the Baptists". A similar increase may be inferred to have taken place in St Thomas-in-the-East, which would account for their high visibility when culprits were sought by the Colonial Government following the Morant Bay Riot four years later.

Myal was not suppressed following the Great Revival as it had been after its lesser manifestations in the 1840s. It was now to be absorbed into the emerging Revival cults of Pocomania and Zion. Revivalists, known as such, have continued since the Great Revival. For a larger number the Pentecostal churches from the USA were to provide the practices in worship most favoured in Jamaica. In the 1860s, however, the native Baptists developed the strongest identifiable groups independent of the European missions, and were proud of their native leadership. An awareness that they were Jamaican born and black led increased their attraction to those who regarded European missionaries as mercenary and strongly tending to align themselves with the Colonial Government, if not the House of Assembly.

The Great Revival marked an unmistakable assertion of Jamaican initiative in their own religious practice. In its stimulation of masses of poor people to demonstrate their own feelings it must have suggested to many of them the need to act on their own behalf in other, secular, matters. It is not surprising that the representations and protests of the 1860s were invariably presented as a righteous cause with a religious justification.

CHAPTER 6

Social Consciences

No friend, I never gave the people bad advice, I only told them the Lord would send them a day of deliverance.
G.W. Gordon, 12 October 1865

By the 1860s, the Christian religious life of the people, in its various forms, was markedly associated with their mixed social experiences in the first quarter of a century of "freedom". The preachers, teachers, clerks and salesmen, with those small farmers who had found viable markets, in the main formed the respectable congregations of the mission chapels; there they established their own goals and influence. Longer term "middle class" groups, predominantly white and coloured, marked their place in society by joining the Established Church, soon to be disestablished, and in smaller numbers the Roman Catholic groups where they were developing. The majority of the population preferred Afro-Jamaican forms of Christianity derived from native Baptist and independent Methodist groups, with a variety rising from the individual initiatives of many Jamaican deacons, leaders and preachers who had created their own local churches. Many of the Jamaican led groups had broken from mission chapels for different reasons and prided themselves on associating their religious practices with true Jamaican aspirations.

In a free Jamaica, membership of a religious group was essentially a social advantage whether in establishing status in the European derived denominations or in the mutual benefits of small native groups. Where chapel or church membership did not meet the capabilities or the desires of the people they withdrew from the missions to reconstruct religious

Social Consciences

practices and promote their own survival in adversity. In developing their own self-contained Christian communities, without central organisation, Jamaican people felt that they had a resource for expressing local needs and in the final outcome for taking action on their own behalf.

In one fundamental respect all Christian groups now shared a common cause. While slavery continued in the Americas it was actively opposed by mission and native groups alike. In 1839 an anti-slavery group was formed in Jamaica. This was prompted by a communication from the British Anti-Slavery Society seeking the cooperation of their friends in the colonies. Specifically the British society recommended action to ensure that any slave entering British territory anywhere should immediately be freed. Jamaican support for this cause was emphatic, to the fury of the American Consul who regularly reported the freeing of American slaves from American ships in Jamaican ports. They were declared free without delay in petty magistrates' courts, on occasion after they had been borne there by those termed by the consul "worthless and Baptist tampered negroes".[1]

Not only was action taken on Jamaican soil, but the consul frequently warned his government against missionaries travelling to the United States to assist the anti-slavery movement there.[2] On occasion he even warned of the dangers of invasion of the Southern States by a combined force of blacks from Jamaica and Haiti. In any event he urged that missionary travellers should be watched and their luggage searched for subversive literature. These measures were critically important in the consul's opinion "as this class of persons are notorious for their machinations and meddling propensities to enlighten the Negro population".[3]

Most troublesome for the consul, however, were the periodic interventions of crowds in Jamaican ports in support of American slaves, which he recognised as empathy between blacks as well as anti-slavery action. Incidents at the wharfside in both Kingston and Port Maria in 1847 forced the consul to urge ships' captains to abandon disputes about the release of slaves from their crews, and to sail away before they were arrested for trying to prevent it.[4] Clearly the American slaves themselves understood their opportunities for freedom in Jamaica. One jumped out of the boat taking him back to his ship and was not dragged back because there was "such a concourse of persons" who had assembled in his support at the Port Maria wharf. "I am now on the shore of Jamaica, and I claim to be free," he declared as he waded out of the water to the enthusiastic reception of the crowd.⁵ On another occasion "a violent crowd of Negroes and Mulattoes" gathered on the wharf in Kingston to insist on the landing of two black stowaways understood to be held in irons on an American ship in harbour; to avoid further contention the captain gave them up. They were indeed two runaway slaves from Charleston.⁶

Perhaps the most emphatic demonstration of popular anti-slavery occurred in Savanna-la-Mar in 1855 when local people took to their canoes to board an American ship and forcibly release a slave who had not been allowed on shore. The crowd carried him straight to the courthouse where the magistrate forthwith declared him free. He explained his own contribution to his liberation simply. "Hearing that this was a free country I tried to get here," he told his supporters.⁷

It is not possible to quantify the number of American blacks liberated into Jamaican society during the 1840s and 1850s. The American Consul's worried despatches suggested that it was a matter of hundreds. He certainly advised ships' captains to avoid arriving in Jamaica with black crew on board. After the Savanna-la-Mar affair he foresaw that the abduction of black sailors would become commonplace. He further advised collectors of customs in American ports "to prevent Negroes from being cleared out on board our vessels as they scarcely ever fail to desert".⁸

The two elements in the situation frequently noted by the American Consul were, firstly, that Jamaican blacks felt instinctive solidarity with other blacks, slave or free; secondly that attitudes towards freedom were religiously inspired, or "Baptist tampered", as the consul had it. The records show that the dissenting missionary bodies all supported anti-slavery societies everywhere. It seems likely, however, that the spontaneous crowds at the sea ports were native Baptists as much as BMS followers. The group approach and the practical action on an agreed procedure bear the hallmarks of their application to the evils of this world as a socio-religious obligation.

The direct effect on the religious life of the island of the arrival of a number of American blacks can only be surmised. In the ports where they were received there were nonconformist mission stations similar in outlook to the chapels of the Southern States, although overwhelmingly in the care of European pastors; these would welcome new members accustomed to nonconformist moral discipline. It must be assumed, however, that many of the black Americans, now ex-slaves, had been members of black led chapels and/or engaged in the activities of the "invisible institution" of Afro-American religion, so fully described by Albert Raboteau in his *Slave Religion*. The native Baptist and other independent groups must therefore have provided the most familiar religious home for most American ex-slaves in Jamaica. If, as seems probable also, American black Baptist influence had continued, particularly in the western parishes, their groups would have welcomed new arrivals.

It seems a fair assumption that Jamaicans who welcomed black Americans were coming to understand that black solidarity was not only a resource to free those still enslaved, but could also be used for their betterment in a society now free of slavery, but rife with socioeconomic differences based on colour. The rallying calls of Paul Bogle in St Thomas-in-the-East in 1865 summoned up a black solidarity which had strengthened through the postemancipation experiences of ex-slaves and their descendants and was expressed in their socio-religious communities.

A proclamation posted in Lucea in June 1865 demonstrates the interdependence of religious activity and social protest; it also suggests an American element in the group producing it.[9] It was signed by "A Son of Africa" and gives every indication that it was composed by native Baptists. In the long tradition of spirit guidance the writer was inspired by "a voice speaking to him". The Voice instructed its hearers to tell "the sons and daughters of Africa that a great deliverance will take place for them from the hand of the Opposition". Magistrates, proprietors and merchants were identified as the oppressive opposition. The people were to "sanctify themselves for the day of deliverance". Failing this, the Voice would bring a sword into the land "and the sword would come from America". This intriguing reference to America as a final resort for resisting oppression may have been prompted by the recent emancipation of American slaves; but whatever the inspiration it supports the idea that poor Jamaicans at least were well aware of Americans in comparable circumstances to themselves and saw the prospect of united action.

The events leading up to the Morant Bay riot, and its sequel, demonstrated religious attitudes and the varying religious responses of all concerned. Above all, it showed how many Jamaicans had developed a social conscience concerning their own affairs. In one context this was partly the outcome of British nonconformist attitudes emanating from the missionary chapels; even more it appears as the expression of an all-Jamaican reasoned protest against prevailing conditions, offering solutions of their own. It is clear that much of the general opinion forming occurred in the religious communities of both missionary chapel and native Christian groups.

Localised opinions took islandwide form in 1865 following the distribution of the Underhill Letter sent to the Secretary of State in January of that year.[10] Underhill was Secretary of the BMS and had visited Jamaica, at the insistence of the BMS missionaries, a few years earlier. The first articulated protest of the year therefore came from a missionary impetus. Underhill meetings, which produced many resolutions from gatherings throughout the island, were prompted by the Governor's distribution of the letter when it arrived in Jamaica. Missionary participation in the meetings varied considerably according to individual choice. There can be no doubt, however, that their congregations and great numbers from the native Christian groups constituted the large attendance at each meeting. The utterances of George William Gordon, who addressed many of the meetings, drew on the religious experience of his hearers. "Call on your ministers to reveal your true condition, and then call on heaven to witness and have mercy," he urged the assemblage at St Ann, advising them to deal with "men with a sense of right and wrong who can appreciate you". Similarly at the St Thomas-in-the-East meeting he gave a religious imperative to his message in begging the people to help themselves, "then heaven will help you". What the established authorities regarded as incitement was far more in the tradition of the native preacher. "Remember that he only is free whom the truth makes free", admonished Gordon again, "you are no longer slaves but free men; then as free men act your part."[11]

Underhill in his *Tragedy of Morant Bay* later reported on other less eminent speakers at the meetings. He referred in particular to Samuel Holt and Samuel Clarke, converts to Christianity, who had been educated to become preachers. "The very diction of the sacred volume had become to them their mother tongue", wrote Underhill, "they were leaders among their brethren, loyal to the Queen, lovers of law and order, peaceable and peace loving."[12] It can be assumed that the majority addressing the Underhill meetings presented a righteous, Christian cause, with biblical references and due respect for constituted authority in Jamaica and Britain. Furthermore their hearers, educated and uneducated, understood the message and could participate in supporting the resolutions sent in by each meeting. The response was the outcome of both mission led

Christian teaching and that of native Christian principles of social action, on this occasion unusually joined in common cause.

The Underhill Letter correctly identified the nature and the causes of the widespread distress of the time. The same proposals as were made by the people themselves were also advocated by Underhill, namely making more land available for the growing of staples, particularly sugar, cotton and coffee. According to Underhill such favourable incentives could attract a new generation of investors to the island. In a petition to the Queen from the Poor People of St Ann's Parish the same point is made, but not for more overseas investors; significantly these small cultivators asked for land to develop new crops themselves. "If our most Gracious Sovereign Lady will be so kind as to get a quantity of land, we will put our hands and heart to work, and cultivate coffee, corn, canes, cotton and tobacco, and other produce," the petitioners proposed.[13] The need to diversify export crops was entirely clear to the poor people of St Ann; their difference from Underhill was that they saw the development as favouring a Jamaican smallholding agricultural industry rather than a new wave of overseas investment in large-scale plantation agriculture. Representations from St Thomas-in-the-East under Paul Bogle had a similar design in seeking access to the backlands, mainly Crown Lands, in that parish.

The ministers of the Jamaica Baptist Union wrote independently to the Governor during 1865. They were less concerned with specific economic developments than with the poor local provisions which depressed living standards, and consequently affected the moral outlook of the people. They deplored, of course, those factors of family life which had divorced the majority of the people from the chapels on definition. The matters raised by the missionaries did indeed underline the dilemmas of the large marginalised population. They criticised lack of medical services for the poor; the want of any poor law or legal provision for illegitimate children or the aged; the inadequate provision for the orphans created by the epidemics of 1850-52; above all they deplored the lack of control over the growing numbers of illegitimate children leaving home at twelve or thirteen years of age to become the young criminals now filling the gaols. The ministers of the Jamaica Baptist Union described the decline of respectability, which had been the hallmark of their influence in Jamaican society, and the dire consequences to be anticipated, as follows:

People who, when they could dress with propriety, were in the habit of regularly attending public worship on the Lord's Day, and of contributing cheerfully for religious services, and who were in the habit of sending their children to school, are now disregarding these duties and permitting their offspring to grow up in ignorance that must be productive of the most serious evils.

The JBU pastors went on to bemoan the fact that, despite all their preaching and teaching, parents were failing to bring up their children "in habits of obedience, industry, self respect and honesty". Instead the young people left home at an early age, associated with bad neighbours and developed "a reckless, lawless and roving disposition"; the inevitable consequence was a life of crime.[14] The JBU ministers' description of the young people of the 1860s coincides with the strictures fourteen years later of *The Report of the Commission on the Juvenile Population* which described juvenile vagrancy, the drift of young people to the towns and their decline into prostitution and crime. The young people born in the postemancipation decades were in large number totally indifferent to the missionary culture; it did not in their opinion address their circumstances or their critical struggle for survival. In 1865 the JBU ministers in Jamaica recognised the "juvenile culture" which was emerging, but had no new prescriptions to offer.

The WMMS missionaries maintained their tradition of noninvolvement in Jamaican politics. They did, however, despatch their views on the Underhill Letter to their home society in London. Apart from the veteran, Isaac Whitehouse who, nearly forty years after defending his slave members in St Ann's Bay, wrote to disassociate himself from both the Underhill Letter and the meetings that followed, most of the other long-standing WMMS missionaries showed considerable sympathy with the people. In particular, Chairman Edmondson, now thirty years in the office, replied to the Colonial Secretary on receiving the Underhill Letter. He opened by saying that this was his first political statement since he had arrived in the West Indies forty years earlier. He agreed with Underhill's analysis, but injected modifications of attitude and additional points which revealed the observations of the man on the ground. In summary his conclusions on the state of the population were:

1. That the people were not so much denied access to the courts, but that they did not receive as much consideration there as they had

done from the Stipendiary Magistrates.
2. That the distress was very great, especially for the old and the sick. People were not coming to church or school because they lacked clothing.
3. Larceny and immorality were the result of the conditions.
4. Although the majority were in great distress, a promising minority had improved their circumstances and were "likely to rise to respectability".
5. Private capital should be raised and land tenure should be regulated so that much more land could be rented out.
6. Education should include the teaching of agriculture "with such machinery as science is producing for the better cultivation of the soil".
7. Railways should be built.
8. Disestablishment of the Established Church would release new public revenue for social expenditure.
9. Above all the people were very ready to work hard for fair wages.[15]

Edmondson retained the missionary attitude that wage employment was the prime need, that private capital should be attracted to provide it and of course that "respectability" was the desired outcome. He did, however, recognise that an important minority had bettered themselves by their own initiatives and that the people were very ready to work hard given the opportunity. Edmondson's comments counteracted the widespread condemnation of a so-called idle and immoral people. Methodism might have retained more followers at this stage had such views been more publicly stated; the policy of neutrality did nothing to promote the WMMS chapels in hard times.

Another, belated, response to the Underhill Letter came from Gardner, the senior LMS missionary of the time. His interest was very particular and was explained in a letter to the governor in October 1865, immediately following George William Gordon's execution. Gardner felt a special need to disassociate himself from what he regarded as Gordon's revolutionary principles because Gordon had been a member of the Kingston LMS chapel until some four years previously; his widow still was. Gardner explained that Gordon had since adopted an "erratic" religious practice of his own, including himself preaching and administering the Lord's Supper in various native Baptist chapels. Also he had much associated with "Mr Fletcher", formerly Presbyterian according to Gardner; this was of course Duncan Fletcher, the LMS missionary who had earlier been criticised for his public expression of social views. These LMS connections with Gordon clearly distressed Gardner who felt that "he was promulgating extreme revolutionary principles". His now retrospective comment on the Underhill Letter was that he did not deny that the people had grievances, but he strongly disapproved of the fact that "the subject had been made a handle by political agitators".[16] Gardner's interpretation of the activities at the Underhill meetings was shared by a substantial number of other missionaries of all societies in Jamaica. They feared the public expression of discontent, saw it as political agitation and associated the native Baptists with the unrest. They certainly reflected Governor Eyre's opinions, even if they did not influence them.

The resolutions of Underhill meetings and the independent petitions of 1865 were community led, not missionary led, although individual missionaries, particularly JBU ministers such as Edward Hewett and the Jamaican Edwin Palmer, promoted the meetings and the dispatch of their resolutions. However, the resolutions were written in standard Victorian English which suggests that logistical help was sought from, if not missionaries themselves, their associates and the products of their schools. From Spanish Town, for example, the Underhill meeting resolved "that this Meeting views with alarm the distressed condition of nearly all classes of the people of this Colony, from want of employment in consequence of the abandonment of a large number of estates, and the staple of the country being no longer remunerative, caused by being brought into unequal competition with slave grown produce". The Spanish Town resolutions also drew attention to the growing threat of emigration to the economy, by the departure of the most skilled workers from the island.

The Hanover meeting resolutions more baldly stated "that very decided measures of relief are now imperatively demanded" although the proposers would deprecate "the bestowal of eleemosynary aid, as calculated still further to degrade and pauperise the people". They resolved that relief from heavy taxation would be a more suitable way of tackling the problem of poverty. These resolutions and their analyses, are not the product of an ignorant and excitable people as so often described by British commentators.[17]

Social Consciences

Petitions from the Poor People of St Ann and from Paul Bogle and his followers in Stony Gut, presented in June and October 1865 respectively, were not written in Victorian English. They were simple and clear statements, in both cases emphasising that they were the Queen's loyal subjects, presenting their problems directly. Where the "Poor People of St Ann" quite respectfully petitioned for more land as the solution of their problems, the "petitioners of St Thomas-in-the-East" were protesting against a specific incident in the magistrate's court, and so displayed more militancy in their pleas for protection. If refused, they warned, "we will be compelled to put our shoulders to the wheel, as we have been imposed upon for a period of 27 years with due obeisance to the laws of our Queen and country, and we can no longer endure the same".[18] These were communications from grassroots Jamaicans reflecting on their actual experience in the postemancipation era and on different specific issues. They asked for conditions and rights to give them status as independent and free British citizens. This was not the same set of values as "the obedience, industry, self respect and honesty" required of them in the JBU statement. Rather they sought conditions to assert their own values and to work for their own families and communities in their own way.

Paul Bogle and his followers were native Baptists meeting and planning their representations in the chapel that they had built for themselves a few months earlier. It can be assumed that a large proportion of the Poor People of St Ann were likewise native Baptists, or independent Methodists since this had been a stronghold of the Pennockites in former years. In short the independent Jamaican Christian groups had found a voice which could now communicate with the authorities, if not in their form of the language, most certainly in a clear and direct English to state their own concerns unmistakably.

In St Thomas-in-the-East, where the outbreak occurred in October 1865, no doubt fortuitously missionary pastors were nearly all Jamaicans. The four WMMS missionaries were all natives of the country, as was one of the two LMS pastors; the only JBU minister was in the extreme north of the parish, and was in any case away at the time of the trouble. The near absence of European missionaries was explained by the unhealthy nature of the parish especially in Morant Bay itself where there had been considerable mortality in missionary families over the years. It would be hard to say whether their scarcity was also occasioned by the prevalence of native Baptist communities in the parish, or was the cause of it. These were well established and had taken root with an intercommunication facilitated by their proximity to each other. There are two indications that the parish was regarded by Gordon, who owned two properties there, as a field for a native Baptist mission. In a letter to Bogle in 1864 he remarked that he was writing on a fast day and felt moved to itemise the purposes of these traditional days in the native Baptist practice. The last item in his list was "To bless Mr Warren in the Word and in his mission to St Thomas-in-the-East."[19] Mr Warren was the preacher at the chapel built by Gordon at Spring, his estate abutting onto Stony Gut. Mr Warren and Gordon himself certainly preached at Stony Gut and other native Baptist meeting places in the parish, as part of a regular interchange of preachers between the settlements.

The second indication that Gordon at least contemplated a wider organisation for the native church was contained in the charge to Paul Bogle when he was ordained deacon in Gordon's Tabernacle in Kingston. Signed by Gordon as "secretary", the certificate called upon the new deacon "in all things to be obedient to the rules of the Church devoting himself through the Grace of God faithfully to the work".[20] This was apparently the first suggestion that the native Baptists were growing into a collective church with "rules". Although these communications were essentially about the religious life of the native Baptists they also implied a concern for secular affairs as an aspect of religious observance. It is worth quoting Gordon's agenda for prayer and contemplation on a fast day more fully to illustrate the point:

> Today is a fast day – to call to mind our sins.
> To implore God to grant us mercies and to help us in our necessities.
> To bless our relations and our friends.
> To *pardon our enemies*.
> To take away the reproach of sin from our Land.
> To bless all Lands with the light of Gospel truth.
> To grant prosperity to our Cause for His Glory in this city.[21]

The contrast between this guide to prayer on a fast day and the missionary version of native Baptist religious observance is striking. Gordon accepted clearly the doctrine of personal and collective sins and the need to pray for God in his mercy to forgive. But also God is asked "to help us in our necessities" and to bless relatives and friends. Enemies are to be pardoned. The well-known Jamaican support for missions abroad is recognised and prosperity for "our Cause for His Glory" at home is implored. In short the Christian tenets with the omission of hellfire and retribution, are similar to most of the contemporary nonconformist preaching of the missions.

So far as their poverty allowed, the people of St Thomas-in-the-East were also trying to adopt some of the symbols of "respectability" usually associated with the mission chapels. Most of these communities had built their own meeting houses and some had sizeable chapels, as at Stony Gut. They had literate preachers and leaders emerging in their midst; a large Bible was the centrepiece of their meeting house decor. Some members could now even "keep Sunday dress". But in addition to these externals in St Thomas-in-the-East there was mutual support, not only within the communities, but also between them. This was expected by Bogle in the days immediately before the disturbance in Morant Bay.[22] He was able to send for recruits from the other native Baptist settlements for his band of protesters gathering in Stony Gut Chapel; in the twelve days before he was caught in Hayfield he must have been sheltered on the run amongst the same communities. The pursuing military and Maroons certainly thought so, and inflicted drastic punishment throughout the parish in the month of martial law following the riot in Morant Bay.

Neither the Christian doctrinal concerns of the native Baptists, nor their group solidarity were appreciated by their critics in the missions and in the colonial establishment. Ross, the LMS teacher/catechist in Morant Bay, was one who promoted a negative view of the parish. He reported that it was behind the rest of the island religiously, educationally and socially. "Illicit intercourse" and "love of dress prevailed", he insisted; though he must have known that this was hardly exclusive to St Thomas-in-the-East. The clue to the alleged backwardness lay no doubt in Ross's further explanation of why he could make little headway in Morant Bay, namely that "the religion of the Bible is not the religion of the inhabitants".[23] That a similar illiteracy prevailed perforce throughout the colony did not prevent it remaining a special charge against native Baptists and the main reason for finding them religiously, educationally and socially inferior to followers of missionary led churches. When in addition they were classed as "political agitators" much of the Euro-Christian element in the Jamaican community could be expected to condemn their compatriots first as protesting petitioners and then as rioters. This was not simply the difference between Euro-Christian and Afro-Christian principles; it was as much the difference between the missionary social culture and Jamaican grass roots protest, both derived from Christian appeals for justice and order.

Examples of response to the Morant Bay riot reported by the missionaries illustrate the differences which had emerged among the Jamaican people at large, influenced by their different experiences of the Christian religion. Several missionaries in other parts of the island reported the shame and shock of their members concerning events in St Thomas-in-the-East. "Thousands of blacks, loyal blacks, are ashamed of their countrymen, and have wept over the fiendish actions of their deluded brethren", reported the missionary at Mount Zion. Many were saying, he continued, "What will Mrs. Queen and kind Christian friends in England think of us now? We have free; what more do we want? We can't do without the White people."[24] The veteran, Whitehouse, was similarly complacent about the loyalty of the St Ann Methodists; the regrettable petition from "the Poor People" of the parish had been Baptist inspired, he claimed.[25] In Mandeville Alloway's deacons entirely disassociated themselves from "the rebellion" and enrolled as special constables in the Volunteer Corps. The missionary in consequence no longer feared attacks from "lawless savages". He further quoted a letter from one of his members now working in Kingston. His correspondent was "ashamed that in our land comparatively full of Ministers and teachers, and possessing so many Bibles, there could be found men capable of committing, and willing to commit, such dreadful crimes as have stained our island's history".[26]

At First Hill the missionary was similarly reassured by the presence of troops at Falmouth. He also reported the outrage of his members at "the atrocities" committed by their countrymen. He was not himself, however, surprised by the turn of events because he had noted for the past two years, particularly among young people, "a growing up a want [sic] of respect for their Rulers, both civil and religious".[27] This was an outright assumption that European missionaries could be equated with the colonial authorities as "rulers". The many native Baptists of the district, a people sorely neglected by the civil rulers, would not have appreciated a European pastor's association with the authorities, nor probably have adopted his members' attitude to the news from St Thomas-in-the-East.

Social Consciences

These examples show that among the missionaries throughout the island there was a real fear of a rebellion of blacks against the white establishment, which many thought included themselves. Secondly, according to their accounts, their chapel leaders and members deplored the threat and were upset about what the Queen and the British supporters of their chapels would think of them. Thirdly, at least their initial response was a far greater horror concerning reported atrocities at Morant Bay than any condemnation of the subsequent harsh and parishwide retribution under martial law. They must soon have been disconcerted to find that the latter in fact was what disturbed that section of the British public whose good opinion they were so anxious to maintain. Clarke in Four Paths, who had now spent thirty years as an LMS missionary interestingly wrote about "the dreadful calamity that has come upon us as a People"; he obviously adopted common cause with at least his respectable Jamaican followers. He was moved to repeat early rumours that children's hands had been chopped off by the rebels, ministers wounded, their property burnt, and that one had had his tongue cut out by a woman. These were the actions, he asserted of "an Ignorant and superstitious class of men, Native Baptists".[28] Even Gardner passed on the rumour that Custos Kettelholt's fingers had been cut off so that he could "write no more lies to the Queen".[29]

A more balanced, though alarmist, account was provided by Edmondson reporting the news from Kingston. He described "the awful rebellion" in St Thomas-in-the-East as a long-plotted scheme to kill all the whites and coloureds and seize their land and property. It had been the first object of the rebels in Morant Bay to kill the Custos and the Rector. Now the Governor had declared martial law and had himself sailed to Morant Bay carrying George William Gordon with him. There was a $2,000 reward for the capture of Paul Bogle, "a native Baptist preacher". In Kingston three ministers had been arrested and the disaffected were threatening to burn down the city "if Gordon and the parsons be hanged". The arrested ministers were the Rev Edwin Palmer, a black BMS pastor and a Calabar graduate, the Rev Z.H. Cole, native Baptist minister of the Kingston Tabernacle, and the Rev James Roach, a breakaway independent Methodist pastor. Edmondson's use of their minis- terial title in each case indicates that the native Baptist and independent Methodist ministers were now respected figures in Kingston, despite the authorities' fear of them. They certainly had vocal supporters in their time of need.

Edmondson's personal assessment of the situation was that "although in general a quiet and peaceable race", the black population had been stirred up by the demagogues who addressed the Underhill meetings. He supported the current theory that it was "native preachers, chiefly of the Baptist persuasion" in every parish, who were behind the plotting. They were "utterly incapable of instructing the people in the great principles of gospel truth, and it is highly probable that they have dwelt much on the claims of *classes*, and represented the *Blacks* as an oppressed race who ought to defend themselves".[30] Edmondson's analysis suggests that the long-established native Baptist groups in Kingston might well have been discussing the prevailing economic distress in the political terms he described.

To what extent the issue was consciously one of colour it is hard to say. The whites were certainly a target for rhetoric amongst Baptist protesters, but largely in their roles as magistrates, employers and landholders. Because, however, the majority of European missionaries thought that all whites were at risk, this became the substance of their letters back to Britain. Yet their own random quotation of native Baptist utterances indicated that the contention was more one of native rights against exploitation by authorities from overseas with no stake in the island. Insofar as these protesters included missionaries and clergy in the criticism, it was because of their own tendency to equate themselves with other white residents and "birds of passage". Edmondson quoted the kind of sentiment expressed by native leaders as follows, "You are black and I am black, and you ought to support your own colour. The Blacks are seven to one of the others and they ought to have the island." He does not attribute the utterance to any particular native Baptist and it would have had to be a school educated one to use this language. It was most probably a paraphrase of what Kingston "respectables" were saying about their black countrymen. The petitioners for land and justice in the magistrates' courts did not initially refer to themselves as black. Not until resistance had become active in St Thomas-in-the-East did the call for blacks against whites emerge; the police who tried to arrest Paul Bogle in Stony Gut the day before the riot were certainly urged to join their own kind, and recruiting pleas to other native Baptist communities in the parish were on the same lines. Only from several missionaries, and Governor Eyre, do we hear that this was the basis of an islandwide plot to seize the land.

Two influential European missionaries considerably modified their views before the end of 1865. Gardner, despite his early condemnation of the riot, was much disturbed by the severity of its suppression. Writing in December, he knew of no proof that an islandwide outbreak had ever been intended; nor did he think that the "rebels" ever saw themselves as rising against the Queen. He pointed out that, although "upwerd of one thousand negroes" had been killed in the suppression, not a single soldier or sailor had even been wounded. To amend his previous record he stated that the rebels were not representative of the whole of the St Thomas-in-the-East population, and St Thomas was not a representative parish. He concluded that it would take generations to bring "a civilising influence" to bear where "countless ages of African superstition have left a deep impress".[31] Gardner was never reconciled to the native Baptists who had been the largely successful rivals to the LMS Mission wherever it worked. Nevertheless he could in time modify his view of the events of late 1865 and deplore the overreaction of the retribution. He also joined several others in pressing for an independent investigation into the affair.

There were missionaries who did not share their colleagues' alarmist reactions to the events of 1865. John Mearns, soon to take over unwillingly as Chairman of the Methodist mission to Jamaica, wrote throughout 1865 more liberally than most, from his station at Montego Bay. In May he approved of the Underhill meetings as the only opportunity for people to present their dire problems. He assured the WMMS that neither the Underhill Letter nor the people's own resolutions in any way exaggerated conditions in Jamaica. For good measure he claimed that the Baptists were trying to help their impoverished followers and it was time that the Methodists did the same.[32] Immediately on the news of the Morant Bay Riot in October, Mearns doubted that there would be any sequel elsewhere in the island.[33] By December he was sure there had been "no organised rebellions" and that "much blood had been wantonly shed by Governor Eyre". Furthermore, he added two more opinions. Firstly that George William Gordon had been "cruelly murdered" and, secondly that "we need a different kind of government from what we have, and something more akin to justice than anything we have yet had." He concluded with the information that he had joined with the BMS and Presbyterian missionaries in St James in a petition to the Queen for a full commission of enquiry into the Morant Bay affair and its aftermath.[34]

It is noticeable that Mearns used "we" in the communication, and thus conveyed the impression that he was identifying himself with Jamaican interests. He had worked in the island for twenty-five years already. He was committed to the development of a native ministry and will later be seen as a backer of the Jamaican W. Clarke Murray, in his representations from Bath on the effects there of the reprisals following the riot. It is not surprising that Mearns hoped that the WMMS would not announce his appointment to the chairmanship before the upcoming district meeting. He anticipated two sets of opponents: the older colleagues who would dislike his views on the events of the previous year; he also thought that the native WMMS missionaries would prefer a non-European chairman.

If the European missionary response to the riot and its sequel ranged from condemnation of native savagery to revulsion for the official repression, it must be said that the reactions of the Jamaican pastors in the missions were somewhat of the same contradictory order. Lindo, now at Porus, after a long career as schoolmaster/catechist in Morant Bay, was most anxious to distance himself from events in St Thomas-in-the-East and to insist on the essentially respectable nature of the vast majority of Jamaicans at large. Writing to the *Missionary Magazine and Chronicle* in January 1866, he sought to allay any British doubts concerning his people's character. He assured his British readers that Jamaican chapel members were drawn from "the industrious, honest and respectable portion of the peasantry". He equated "their consistent Christian character and improved social position" as a convincing illustration that "Godliness is profitable in all things, having promise of the life that now is and of that which is to come." As a Jamaican assertion of the European Protestant work ethic of progress by works in faith, Lindo's cannot be bettered. In case his readers failed to appreciate the Jamaican connection with missionary culture he regaled them with the members' impressive appearance on the Sabbath and on special occasions. They could witness, if they came to Jamaica, "numbers of well dressed persons", many on horseback, female riders in cloth habits and males in cloth coats, "tweeds, silk mantles, parasols, crinolines, feathers, flowers, gloves and ribbons, all in fine and tasteful exhibition". If ever a connection between chapel membership and aspirations for social prestige was required, Lindo had provided it, all in the interests of rejecting any association with the motives of his compatriots who, in his opinion, had protested too vigorously in St Thomas-in-the-East. Unhappily for his case Lindo also had to admit that a much larger proportion of his countrymen, and chiefly the young people, were what he called "indolent and wilfully ignorant". St Thomas-in-the-East was particularly backward and educationally destitute. On information received from his earlier sphere of operations Lindo concluded that "the leaders of the outbreak were men of some property and intelligence who incited the mass of ignorant and deluded creatures against the authorities, and employed them to do their bidding".[35] He did not, however, refer to any islandwide plot and he too asserted the need for an independent enquiry.

The reactions of the Jamaican missionaries stationed in St Thomas-in-the-East are particularly interesting. It is striking that none of them anticipated any danger of an islandwide sequel to the events in the parish where they worked. Parnther, the Jamaican Methodist missionary in Morant Bay, remained there throughout. He sheltered the Rector's family in his mission house. He witnessed much of the town riot of men and women with "rifles, cutlasses, bludgeons and other destructive weapons" and he observed the prompt arrival of the troops and their activities during martial law. His members and hearers were scattered; some were arrested though he did not know whether they were in fact guilty of participation in the riot.[36] Parnther was increasingly distressed by the punitive activities of the troops and of the Maroons who had been recruited to capture rebels; he reported that they were "flogging and executing the rebels at a fearful rate and scouring the countryside for others".[37] By the end of the year he hoped for an enquiry because he thought that the causes of the riot were more complex than was stated publicly, and that the Maroons and the soldiers had attacked black people indiscriminately.[38]

Alexander Foote escaped from Manchioneal with his family and took refuge on an American ship anchored at Port Antonio. He made it clear that it was the ferocity of the troops rather than fear of any rebels which had driven him from his station. Their severity could in his opinion, only be justified by dread of a much greater rebellion. He held the same view as Lindo, that it was the ignorant poor who were responsible for the riot at Morant Bay.[39]

William Harty, the Jamaican LMS missionary at Prospect, alone of the St Thomas-in-the-East pastors, accepted the policy of the colonial authorities and thought that the severe repression was justified. He blamed the native Baptists stating that in St Thomas-in-the-East they were by no means poor, and had used their chapels and meeting places as "dens of sedition".⁴⁰ Harty in fact got into dire trouble with his members for what they regarded as partisan activity during martial law. He had given shelter to the wife of an overseer who had fled from his estate; she had carried her husband's gun with her; a small party of LMS members came to collect the gun. Harty reported them to the constables and gave evidence against them at their court martial; they were all executed. The missionary's stated problem when writing of the event was that the victims' parents and friends were very resentful and he was thinking of expelling them for their hostile attitude.⁴¹ As a response to the occasion this could hardly have been more unsympathetic or unproductive for the future of the station. As a Jamaican he must have seemed particularly faithless to his members, bereaved through his instrumentality. Accusations of treason were made on both sides.

Harty undoubtedly remained the most partisan of the missionaries on the side of the colonial authorities. His last record in the LMS papers is a personal address to Sir John Peter Grant, the first governor under the Crown Colony government introduced after the troubles. Harty informed his new governor that he had not previously been concerned with politics but would now like to advise on "the moral, social and religious progress of our people" upon which he claimed to have strong convictions.⁴² There is no evidence that his offer was ever taken up. His convictions would certainly not have been representative of those of other missionary pastors of 1866, least of all the Jamaican ones.

The most sustained Jamaican missionary comment on the riot and its sequel came from William Clarke Murray, stationed at Bath since his full connection with the WMMS in 1863. His first response to the news of the riot was not judgmental. He knew that poverty, and no doubt oppression, prevailed in the parish; he doubted whether it merited a riot. What most concerned him at this stage was the distress to the people which would be caused by even less employment on the estates as a consequence of the violent protest.⁴³ Two months later, having now encountered the violence of troops and Maroons in Bath, Murray acted definitively. Very courageously he wrote to the commanding officer objecting to the atrocities against "loyal subjects" perpetrated by his men. The risk he took as a coloured Jamaican pastor under martial law was not a small one. The troops were hounding native Baptist preachers as alleged instigators of a rebellion; four pastors had been brought in chains from Kingston to be tried on charges of being involved in the plot. It was hardly a time to trust in the discrimination of British troops to recognise as different from the others a respectable WMMS Jamaican missionary, protesting against their activities. Murray must have been aware of his precarious position for he marked his report to the WMMS "For the Eyes of the Committee only". He explained that he would be able to write more fully if he were in England; in Jamaica some measures of martial law had been retained to deal with any suspicion of treason, including published opinions. The colonel replying to Murray's letter blamed the Maroons for any excesses and conceded that they had indeed been holding their own court martials without authority. Murray and his wife were insulted in the streets of Bath for his intervention with the authorities, but he was nonetheless satisfied because it "proved a check to Maroon lawlessness".[44]

The same long report to the WMMS also contained Murray's considered judgement on what had occurred in the parish. He dismissed fears of a general rebellion as confined to the Governor and a few officials; he had obviously not yet encountered the alarm of several missionary colleagues. He cited two particular reasons for discontent in Morant Bay. In the first place the Custos had refused the use of the court house for an Underhill Meeting in August; secondly, the only Stipendiary Magistrate, the local people's one hope for impartial justice, had been transferred to Portland. Although he obviously sympathised with these causes, Murray nevertheless thought that the actual riot had been conducted by "lewd fellows of the baser sort led by the political men". He felt that few Methodists had been involved, except for looting; five, however, had been hanged in Bath alone. Murray's full sense of outrage was directed at the suppression of the outbreak with its indiscriminate shootings, hang- ings and floggings, during martial law. In the letter, said to be tempered in case it fell into the wrong hands, he could hardly have been more explicit:

> Escape for a black man was scarcely possible whatever may have been the character of his offence. I feel a thrill of horror as I recall the hasty, and to my mind vindictive, manner in which thousands of souls were hurried into eternity offering no resistance to Her Majesty's troops. As for the atrocities committed by the Maroons the tale would scarcely be credited in enlightened and Christian England.[45]

Murray wrote a "Report on the Religious State of Bath" to be accepted by the District Meeting in January 1866. Its reception showed how little the majority of his colleagues even then shared his views or his sense of outrage about what had happened in St Thomas-in-the-East. They disputed four paragraphs. Two were rejected by a majority vote; one was only passed by the casting vote of the new chairman, Mearns, and the fourth was passed without a vote but with strong objections registered. Each of the paragraphs which met with opposition presented ordinary Jamaican people in a favourable and sympathetic light.[46]

One of the rejected statements simply defended the moral status of those Jamaicans who had been influenced by missionary religion and education. After seventy-four years of the Methodist mission to Jamaica a majority of the current missionaries were not even now prepared to give credit to their own loyal followers.

The other rejected paragraph did indeed refer specifically to recent events. Expressing profound sympathy for those who had experienced loss of life and property the paragraph first stated Murray's view of the missionary dilemma in the circumstances:

> Our position as a Missionary was felt to be peculiar and perplexing, endeavouring to discharge on the one hand our duty to a denounced and seemingly doomed class and, on the other, to escape the tremendous power that sought to crush its victims on every side. We thank God for the help by which we were enabled to steer our dangerous course between the rocks on either side.

This was undoubtedly a true account of Murray's own experience of the events he had faced. It was not accepted by the majority of his colleagues. Nor were they prepared to support a balanced statement expressing disbelief in two extreme interpretations of the rioters' intentions. Firstly, they would not accept Murray's contention that no murder had been contemplated in advance by the rioters. Secondly, they would not support his denial of the view that the black population of the parish were "disposed to throw off British rule and as a preliminary step thereto to make an end to the white and coloured race". It would appear that the majority of the Methodist missionaries, three months after the riot, did still credit these extreme views of the event.

The paragraph retained only by the chairman's casting vote reported that sixty-four Methodist members had been shot or hanged in St Thomas-in-the-East, some for looting, five for conspiracy and others, innocent of any complicity, "were swept away by the appalling strong current of retribution which coursed through the parish". Half the missionaries would not accept this interpretation of the suppression of the people of St Thomas.

Finally, the paragraph retained with strong objection, concerned the fate of a "harmless, loyal and well-beloved" member who had been shot dead by Maroons and his house burnt down in sight of his now destitute wife and family. Several missionaries did not wish to deplore even the sad fate of one of their own members.

The new chairman, Mearns, appalled by the attitudes of over half his colleagues tried to explain them to the WMMS in London. They were trying to prove their loyalty beyond dispute, he suggested. They positively desired to be identified with "the respectable classes" and consequently *"to show that they had no sympathy with the lower orders"*. In his letter enclosing Murray's unedited Bath report Mearns confessed that there was "a great gulph" between himself and half the Methodist mission. He himself was again joining with other dissenting missionaries in St James now requesting that the Royal Commission currently conducting its enquiries should not only examine the deeds of the riot and its suppression; they should also explore "the reasons for the astounding allegation that seditious and murderous designs are entertained by the black population in general" and the abiding belief "that a mighty danger thus threatens the land".[47] Mearns revealed that the majority, of WMMS missionaries at least, retained negative views of the events of 1865 and, worse still, of the "lower orders" whom they regarded as responsible.

The sympathies of both British and Jamaican missionaries clearly remained divided, especially in the WMMS and the LMS missions. There was a loss of public confidence in those who had not supported the Underhill meetings or who had later in the year signed addresses deploring the attitudes of "the religious and liberal press in England" for criticising Governor Eyre's actions in Jamaica.[48] The transfer of first the young and promising Enos Nuttall and then the Jamaican, Alexander Foote, to the ministry of the Anglican Church was no doubt partly influenced by the attitudes of their older colleagues in the Methodist mission; they both, however, had other reasons for leaving the WMMS. The net effect of the events of 1865 and 1866 was that the Methodists lost a lot of popular support due to the reactionary attitudes of half their mainly British missionaries at the time. It would take the initiatives of Jamaicans such as Murray and Geddes, including the foundation of York

Castle School in the 1870s, to rebuild confidence in the Methodist Church.

The Jamaica Baptist Union, on the other hand, fared better both in popular and official esteem after the departure of Governor Eyre. The Underhill Letter was the product of their parent body, largely based on information provided by the ministers in Jamaica. After the riot and its suppression, David East, Principal of Calabar College since 1850, addressed an uncompromising letter directly to the Secretary of State for the Colonies condemning Governor Eyre's actions. He deprecated in particular:

1. The transportation of people from Kingston for trial under martial law at Morant Bay. This included the native ministers as well as George William Gordon.
2. The hunting down of British subjects, as loyal to the Queen as the British subjects who shot them.
3. The wholesale executions.
4. The parading of Maroons as law-keepers, which would revive old animosities.
5. The libel against the peasantry in accusing them of sedition.
6. The activities of the legislature since the incident [including no doubt the attempt to suppress again all dissenting preachers].[49]

The events of 1865, and the responses to them, demonstrated clearly different Christian influences in Jamaica at the time. The Underhill meetings held in most parishes produced well-formulated resolutions to be sent to the British Government requesting attention to the economic plight of the island and the relief of the poor who were, however, not to receive charity which might further "degrade and pauperise them". These were the sentiments of Jamaican British subjects expressed in the language learnt in the chapels and the elementary schools. The formulators had a class attitude separating them from the mass of their own population whose welfare they nevertheless sought to promote. Undoubtedly the subjects of their concern were present at the meetings, and supported the resolutions. Those meetings chaired and/or addressed by George William Gordon, on the other hand, called on the sufferers to act on their own behalf on moral and religious grounds. "Try to help yourselves and heaven will help you", he urged his hearers; "as free men act your part", he said at the St Thomas-in-the-East Underhill meeting. In the event the native Baptists of the parish made their bid to act accordingly.

It is to be noted that the very thorough Jamaica Royal Commission which investigated the Morant Bay Riot and its sequel either did not recognise or chose to ignore the religious impetus in the district protests of October 1865. The commissioners in fact took evidence from many European ministers of religion, from at least two black American independent preachers and from preachers and members of the native Baptist communities in St Thomas-in-the-East. Of the 730 "witnesses" whom they interviewed in the two months that they sat, a considerable proportion, particularly those presenting themselves at the two hearings in the parish itself, belonged to native Baptist groups. Daunted by the language of "uneducated peasants speaking in accents strange to the ear, often in a phraseology of their own . . . and in many cases still smarting under a sense of injuries sustained", the commissioners decided to concentrate strictly on the origin of the outbreak and its sequel; they emphatically declined to consider "the whole range of politics" for years past, nor indeed for the year past. It is the body of the evidence, not the report itself, which reveals the range of attitudes prevailing in the society, and the Christian justification offered for contradictory points of view.

In summary the social attitudes revealed by the Jamaican population during 1865 show a common concern to tackle the prevailing poverty. Those led by the Euro-Christian values presented the case for colonial attention to the interests of free British Jamaican citizens, including a respectable lifestyle for the ever growing poor and destitute classes. The mounting number of native Afro-Christians among the poor and destitute in question literally sought their own worldly salvation in their efforts to assert rights to a stake in the country, through means of livelihood and equal justice in the courts. Both versions of social conscience rested on Christian values applied to the problems of the Jamaican community.

CONCLUSION

The Jamaicanisation of Christianity

In the thirty years following emancipation both main forms of Christian belief in Jamaica had made their mark on the free society. The European missionary effort had failed to mould the ex-slave population into the compliant labour force which they, and the British Government, had hoped that they would achieve through religious instruction. Nor were they alone to be the final agents for the conversion of the people to Christianity. They had, however, between them set up a denominational system of churches and elementary schools to provide for a respectable working class maintaining Euro-Christian moral values; this was the bedrock of an emerging middle class in the future.

At least half the population, on the other hand, had adopted Afro-Christian traditions which had equally made their mark in the postemancipation years. Not only did they promote their own demonstrative practices in worship, but native Baptists and a variety of other independents provided a local focus for community problem solving and, in the long run, organisation for social protest. Afro-Christian groups had taken over the Great Revival in 1861, and demonstrated that by choice popular Christianity was charismatic and pentecostal in its activities. They had also, at least by inference, manifested a preference for Jamaican black leadership. This was the seed bed for Pocomania, Revivalism and Zion as the sects which would further develop the expression of Afro-Christian practices. It was also the natural base for future generations of followers of Bedward, Garvey and the Rastafarians. Visions of the millennium, black awareness and the call for an African homeland were all elements of religious persuasion appealing to the Afro-Christian tradition which had to a considerable extent nurtured them. The African religious roots were as old as slavery; the Afro-Christian tradition dated from 1783, and there remained no central organisation for an ever more complex development of creative religious practices in separate communities. The fact that the groups applied their Christian tenets to their social and economic problems in this world meant that religious beliefs dealing with dilemmas, such as racial discrimination and poverty, were readily accepted. They were, and are, a logical progression in the Afro-Christian tradition.

From the mid nineteenth century the development of the Christian religion in Jamaica can be presented as a kind of counterpoint of movements in the two traditions which gave it birth. European missionaries continued to arrive and well into the twentieth century the formal churches were largely staffed by European clergy and pastors; the emergence of a native ministry in all denominations took a considerable time. The Crown Colony administration, from 1866 onwards, disestablished the Anglican Church and thereafter backed all the formal churches to provide more elementary schools and to establish denominational secondary schools, more as a resource for educational development than as a religious imperative. The Euro-Christian influence was evident in the rise of the middle class as it had been in enabling other "respectable classes" to emerge in the early postemancipation years.

The Revival chapels and the many other variants of Afro-Christian religion produced a wide variety of preachers, leaders, elders, shepherds, who have likewise exercised strong social controls in the lives of their flocks. A case in point has been the vexed question of Christian marriage as a condition of membership. Most Afro-Christian sects have disapproved of polygamy, but accept that monogamy is acceptable without marriage; in short that common-law partnerships are not a sin. This interpretation of monogamy must alone have determined the place of worship of countless Jamaicans deterred by British moral certainties in the Euro-Christian churches.

Christian religious life in whatever form was well rooted by the 1860s. The Bible was by then the centrepiece in Protestant churches and chapels and in the meeting places of the sects alike. Biblical language and phraseology entered into the people's discourse at many levels. It was both the rhetoric of civil leaders and the language of appeal for the grass roots population, and has remained so. The last three Prime Ministers, for example, have been called Joshua, the deliverer and the prophet, respectively. The Old Testament and the Book of Revelations, rather than the Gospels, tend to provide the most vivid metaphors.

It would appear that, although the formal churches became increasingly competitive in opening new places of worship and new schools, the population at large was not primarily denominationally led. The practice of changing churches remained and has tended to follow social determinants. The socially mobile minority has increased modestly over the generations. They have been assisted by such factors in turn as access to the American banana market for small farmers, the experience of returning migrants from employment projects abroad, the return of World War veterans twice in the twentieth century and ultimately the wider opportunities for nationals following political independence in 1962. All these have contributed to a growing and strengthening middle class, the mainstay of the formal churches, and increasingly the products of the secondary schools, denominational and otherwise provided. They were in the main loyal British colonial citizens adopting European mores, interests, and class consciousness – "almost the same, but not white" as Homi Bhabha quotes.[1]

Philip Curtin in his *Two Jamaicas* concluded that the "European Jamaicans" have been preoccupied with economic progress while the "African Jamaicans" have been most interested in religion.[2] This seems by far too broad a generalisation. Every small farmer seeking a viable cash crop or migrant worker returning with his savings to set up a small business has been concentrating on economic progress. He or she may well have signalled that progress by joining, say, the Jamaica Baptist Union chapel or the newly evangelical Anglican Church after its disestablishment. Membership of a Christian body, however, remained central to self-esteem and to social status in the community. Furthermore the leadership, pastoral and lay, has more effectively been determined by the membership in the formal churches. In short, religious allegiance has been linked with social circumstances for the socially mobile and the underprivileged alike.

That religion has been the central concern of African Jamaican communities is indeed also certain. It has remained their essential context for self-expression and social organisation. These communities have not only maintained the charismatic, participatory religious practices which they treasure as their own, they have also been the ready recipients of new preachings, home bred and imported, from the United States in particular. The essential elements continue to be Pentecostal, Revivalist and often millennial and apocalyptic. The "leaders" who were, so to speak, previously "monitors" of missionary chapels have in their own groups become elders, preachers, shepherds and shepherdesses, angels, messengers, embodiments of spirits and, above all in secular terms, brothers and sisters in the Lord. Since there has been no central organisation for these groups there has been ample scope for individual local expression of faith and observance. Myalism has been absorbed into Revivalism; Kumina and Pocomania express the local experience as well as the history of the areas where their rituals are maintained. Numerous Jamaicans who over the colonial years in particular had no role in public life, have played powerful and creative parts in their Christian sects and religious groups. Because religious practices have been conducted in and for the local community they have permeated daily life and social relationships.

The formal churches have by no means been uninfluenced by the African Christian traditions. Noel Erskine's account of his baptism and first communion in his Jamaica Baptist Union church in St Thomas demonstrates the accepted Revivalist influence there.[3] The adoption of rhythmic clapping, drumming, Creole masses and popular music in some Anglican and Roman Catholic services are practices inspired by the same influences. The Jamaicanisation of formal Christian churches draws, at least symbolically, on Afro-Christian traditions, which would have alarmed many of the European missionary fathers of their early years. Christian proselytism since the mid nineteenth century has increasingly come from the United States, often from black churches and congregations; numerically the strongest are the Churches of God. These missions strengthen the pentecostal expression and popular participation favoured by the majority of Jamaican worshippers, and encourage another Jamaican ministry for their chapels.

It is not the purpose of this concluding chapter to deal with the development of Jamaican Christianity since the 1860s. It is rather to show that the equally strong European and African Christian traditions were well established by then, and that their influence fluctuated with the changing socioeconomic fortunes of communities as well as of individuals. The Christian religion was rooted as a motive force to the extent that its manifestations reflected the varying achievements, aspirations and needs of people who depended on religion to deal with the realities of their lives, personal and public. Whether for the middle class Jamaican working in Kingston in the ranks of the colonial civil service allowed to him or for the subsistence cultivator in the villages his religious allegiance, Euro-Christian or Afro-Christian, was his arena for personal recognition, responsible status and self-expression.

The Jamaicanisation of Christian churches was already in 1865 a challenge in store for the European derived denominations. The claims of the first few Jamaican pastors to understand and represent the needs of their own people had already been articulated in the nonconformist churches. The Rev Robert Gordon had already made an issue over his limited acceptability in the Anglican Church.[4] Thomas Geddes, the Jamaican Methodist pastor, had already embarked on his critical "despatches" to the WMMS Committee in London; they developed into acrimony in the 1870s when the "home" missionary society wanted to bar illegitimate boys from the new Methodist secondary school at York Castle. The issues of what Erskine terms "Colonial Christianity" were already joined.

The claims of "native" groups to be the authentic voice of Christian Jamaica were well established by the mid nineteenth century, as exemplified, for example, in the calls of the native Baptists of Mount Zion for the settlement to follow the native preachers, who would stay with the people, rather than the European missionaries who would leave them to return "home".[5] This was a clear antecedent for the Revivalist preacher who years later asked the rhetorical question, "Did you ever see a white preacher west of Slipe Pen Road?"[6] Because native groups have flourished in neglected city areas and isolated villages they have been convinced that they represent Jamaican religion independent of external influences, and have operated accordingly. "Oh yes!" continued the same Revivalist preacher, "we haven't been to no college. We have learned from the spirit", echoes of those who before they could read earlier subordinated the Bible to the spirits.[7] The power of the spirit still energetically demonstrated by the Revivalist's hearers on the same occasion was accompanied by Bible readings and the conventional hymns of the formal churches. The synthesis had been the strong Jamaican contribution to

The Jamaicanisation of Christianity

their own religious expression as more literate generations read and learnt the Word.

Similarly the claims for black interests in Christianity were emphatically made in 1865. Paul Bogle called for black solidarity in his efforts to mobilise support for his protest from the native Baptist communities. His messengers to the other villages called on the black brothers to assemble in Stony Gut Chapel for an enterprise which would be revealed to them there.[8] The constables who came up to arrest Bogle on 10 October, the day before the riot, were not only detained in the chapel, they were also implored to join the party in defence of the interests of their own people. The police leader was induced to take an oath; "You kiss the Book that you join your own colour – so help you God".[9] On the run after the Morant Bay riot Paul Bogle and three associates circulated another appeal for help. "It is time now for us to help ourselves – skin for skin – the iron bars is now broken in this parish," the message ran. "War is at us, my Black skin War is at hand from today to tomorrow," it concluded.[10] Paul Bogle's black awareness in what he regarded as a righteous war in St Thomas-in-the-East was surely a forerunner for the Garvey movement half a century later.

Garvey taught that God created all men equal and that it was a religious duty for black people to strive for "a new world of black men" and ultimately to "triumph in the resurrection of our new born race".[11] The connection between Paul Bogle's initiative in his "Black skin War" and Garvey's movement for independent black action for dignity is clear in its inspiration. Although one was based in a Jamaican parish and the other achieved a "universal" African context, both emphasised a religious authority for their actions.

The Rastafarian movement, born in Jamaica, has probably argued the secular application of religious principle most strongly and topically in the Afro-Christian tradition. Rastafarians have not adopted the guidance of spirits and visions from older Afro-Christian beliefs; they have created a new messianic context based on the religious value of black humanity and the prospect of God's release of an oppressed people. The earlier adoption of Garvey's Back to Africa aspiration has more recently been converted into calls for the Africanisation of Jamaican culture as well as religion. The Rastafarian rejection of a white God is a social as much as a religious response to their experience of twentieth century Christianity; it is clearly in the ever creative tradition of Afro-Jamaican Christianity.

The counterpoint pattern of Christianity in Jamaica, so apparent already by the mid nineteenth century, has by no means died. Christianity developed in Jamaica during two centuries of colonialism. The setting and the moral values were, on the one hand, colonial. On the other hand, a large population lived with little socioeconomic benefit from their colonial status. They used their own initiatives for making a livelihood, often at subsistence levels and they created mutually supportive communities distant in many senses from the preoccupations of the colonial establishment. Their religious life reflected their separation and guided their independent activities. Since Jamaican independence in 1962, the leaders and most of the ministry in the formal churches are Jamaicans. The Jamaica Council of Churches, however, does not embrace the cult religions in the Afro-Jamaican tradition, nor most of the charismatic groups that have come often from black congregations in the United States. The dual Christian heritage remains as the historical legacy of a people who have adopted a religion with enthusiasm, and applied it to a many-faceted experience. Its vitality no doubt springs from confrontation with this world's challenges, as much as from the promises of the next.

Notes

Foreword

1. Shirley C. Gordon, *God Almighty Make Me Free: Christianity in Preemancipation Jamaica* (Bloomington: Indiana Univ. Press, 1996).
2. The Christmas Rebellion in the western parishes, led by Sam Sharpe, was also called the Baptist War by critics holding BMS missionaries responsible. It was in fact organised by native Baptist groups. Described by Mary Turner, *Slaves and Missionaries: The Disintegration of Jamaican Slave Society, 1787-1834* (Urbana: Univ. of Illinois Press, 1982), Chapter 5; and E.K. Brathwaite, "The slave rebellion in the Great River Valley of St James, 1831-32", *Jamaican Historical Review* 13 (1982). Origins discussed S. Gordon, *God Almighty Make Me Free*, Chapter 5.
3. Paul Bogle, leader of the Morant Bay rioters in October 1865, mobilised the protest from the newly built native Baptist chapel in Stony Gut where he was deacon.

Chapter One

1. Arthur Beckwith's evidence to the JRC, 1866, Vol. 413. Beckwith had an independent chapel in St David and was an itinerant preacher in the Blue Mountain Valley. He knew G.W. Gordon and argued with him over the probable effects of the last Underhill meeting, held in Morant Bay in August 1865.
2. British equalisation of duties on all imported sugar caused a prolonged campaign by the plantocracy against unfair competition from slave grown sugar and the consequent encouragement of slavery in Cuba, Brazil and the USA.
3. Cholera, smallpox and yellow fever epidemics occurred in most parts of the island between 1850 and 1852.
4. George Liele was an American slave released by his master after coming to Kingston as an Empire Loyalist in 1783. Already a deacon in black Baptist chapels in South Carolina and Georgia, Liele founded a chapel in Kingston and preached in neighbouring parishes until his death in 1826. Discussed Shirley C. Gordon, *God Almighty Make Me Free: Christianity in Preemancipation Jamaica* (Bloomington: Indiana Univ. Press, 1996), Chapter 3.
5. Moses Baker, a free coloured barber from New York, converted by Liele in Kingston, then hired by a Quaker proprietor to give Christian instruction to his slaves in St James. Over forty years, Baker established a large black Baptist following on the western estates. Discussed Gordon, *God Almighty Make Me Free*, Chapter 3.

6. Paul Bogle, National Hero, deacon of Stony Gut native Baptist Chapel and leader of protests in Morant Bay, culminating in the riot on 11 October 1865.
7. J. Light, Irwin, MMS Papers, 12 April 1818, and F. Gardner's brief for his defence, 1832, BMS Papers.
8. US Consular Despatch, 8 March 1846. Roll 10
9. US Consular Despatch, 15 January 1846. Roll 10
10. US Consular Despatch, 15 November 1847. Roll 10
11. US Consular Despatch, 24 April 1853. Roll 14
12. M. Schuler, *Alas, Alas, Kongo* (Baltimore: John Hopkins Univ. Press, 1980), 104-5.
13. The Mico Institution started as a nondenominational training school in 1836. Denominational training schools were the Moravian Fairfield School, the CMS school at Grove, the BMS Calabar College at Rio Bueno and a Presbyterian school at Montego Bay.
14. "Petition of the poor people of St Ann's Parish", addressed to Queen Victoria in May 1865, and a communication to the Governor from "Petitioners of St Thomas-in-the-East? in October 1865. Both quoted Shirley C. Gordon, *Caribbean Generations* (London: Longman, 1983) 203-4, 205-6.
15. Underhill meetings were held in most parishes to discuss a letter from BMS Secretary Underhill to the Secretary of State for the Colonies, Cardwell, January 1865. It was forwarded to the Governor, Eyre, who distributed copies to custodes and ministers of religion. The meetings sent resolutions to the Colonial Government; some are quoted Gordon, *Caribbean Generations*, 202, 205.

Chapter Two

The Missionary Heyday

1. J.M. Phillippo, *Jamaica: Its Past and Present State* (London 1843), 285-90.
2. The dissenting missions in Jamaica in 1838 were, in order of arrival, the MMS (1754), the WMMS (1791), the BMS (1814), the Presbyterians (1817), the evangelical nondenominational LMS (1834). The CMS was the main missionary arm of the Established Church from 1825. The combined strength of all the missions was less than 50 European ordained missionaries in all, although they were supported by British teachers and catechists in the early postemancipation years.
3. The Colonial Church Union pursued a course of chapel destruction and victimisation of Christian slaves and their missionaries from its inception in February 1832, after the Christmas Rebellion two months earlier, until it was declared illegal in 1834. Compensation for the destroyed chapels was not paid until 1837.
4. Metcalfe to CO, 23 June 1840.
5. Knibb to Gurney 19 July 1844, quoted J. Hinton, *Memoir of William Knibb* (London 1847), 476. For further discussion on the small freeholder franchise encouraged by Knibb see also S. Wilmot, "From Falmouth to Morant Bay: religion and politics in Jamaica, 1838-1865". Paper presented at the Association of Caribbean Historians Conference, Havana, and G. Heuman, *Between Black and White* (Oxford: Clio Press, 1981).

Notes to pages 15–27

Religious Education

6. John Savage, *Report on Education in Jamaica* (1864). Discussed C. Campbell, "Social and economic obstacles to the development of popular education in postemancipation Jamaica", *Journal of Caribbean History* 1 (1970).
7. Wilkinson, Kingston, 17 January 1842, LMS f564.
8. Edmund, Grateful Hill, 26 August 1856, WMMS Jca, f2360.
9. Joyce, Mount Zion, 6 February 1865, LMS f658.
10. Schoolmaster Brown, Mandeville, 30 October 1836, LMS f534.
11. Hodge, Morant Bay, 30 March 1836, LMS f530.
12. *The Brethren's Church in Jamaica for the Past Hundred Years*, 1854, MS Papers.
13. Eastwood, schoolmaster Four Paths, and later student at Ridgemount Academy, "a young man of colour from a notoriously bad family", according to Milne forwarding Eastwood's account, 6 September 1845, LMS f583.
14. Buchner, *The Moravians in Jamaican* (London 1854), 138.
15. Savage, *Report*.
16. Hinton, *Memoir*, 431.
17. Francis Johnson, sent to Clarksonville. John Clarke, *Memorials of Missionary Work in Jamaica* (London 1869).
18. Clarke named seven more Jamaican "native ministers" whom he does not attribute to Calabar, "The Native Ministry" appended.
19. Angus and Wirrell, "Report on visitation to Jamaica", 1846, BMS Papers.
20. Barrett MacLean, Brixton Hill, 8 November 1854, LMS f633.
21. Hall, Ridgemount, 29 September 1851, LMS f608.
22. "Minutes of sub-committee on Ridgemount Academy for training a native ministry in connection with the LMS", 3-4 October 1855, LMS f627.
23. The convert from Four Paths of p. 17 above.
24. "Report on Ridgemount Academy", 1857. LMS f633. Duncan Fletcher became an active sympathiser and biographer of George William Gordon (1867).
25. "Report on Ridgemount Academy", 1858, LMS f636.
26. The latter dropout was Barrett MacLean, see p. 20 above.
27. Gardner, Chapelton 22 May 1855, LMS f626. Gardner was the author of *A History of Jamaica*, 1873.
28. Fletcher, Chapelton, 7 February 1862, LMS f649.
29. Edmondson, Kingston, 18 June, 1863, WMMS Jca., LMS f2386.
30. Resolution of WMMS District Meeting 1864, WMMS Jca. LMS f2389.
31. Nuttall, Kingston, 9 March 1864, WMMS Jca. LMS f2389.

Promotion of Free Villages

32. Phillippo, *Jamaica*, 228.
33. Quoted Hinton, *Memoir*, 486.
34. The subsequent eight-fold expansion in numbers of houses between the censuses of 1844 and 1861 is detailed in UWI's Department of History, *Jamaican Censuses* (Kingston 1980). The largest number of houses built over those years was in St Elizabeth, Westmoreland, Manchester, St Ann and Trelawny " apart from the last named, not parishes strongly serviced by European missionaries.
35. Phillippo, *Jamaica*, 229.
36. Speech in Norfolk, UK, 7 July 1845, quoted Hinton *Memoir*, 485.

37. Discussed by S. Wilmot, "The peacemakers: Baptist missionaries and ex-slaves in western Jamaica, 1838-40", *Jamaican Historical Review* 22 (1982).
38. Characteristics of mission founded free villages discussed by S. Mintz, "The historical sociology of Jamaican villages", *Caribbean Transformations* (Chicago: Aldine Press, 1974).
39. For examples see chapter 3, "Jamaican initiatives in mission chapels".
40. Jones, Mount Providence, March 1843, LMS f571.
41. Buchner, *The Moravians*.
42. Holdsworth to WMMS, Grateful Hill, 5 June 1859, WMMS Jca. f2366.
43. Afro-Caribbean development in a Jamaican free village is discussed in J. Besson, "Family land as model for Martha Brae's new history: culture building in an Afro-Caribbean village" in Carnegie (ed.), *Afro-Caribbean Villages in Historical Perspective* (Kingston: Institute of Jamaica Publications, 1987).

Decline of Missionary Christianity

44. Clarke, Brown's Town, 15 September 1845, BMS Papers.
45. Listed in L. Tucker, *Glorious Liberty* (London 1914).
46. Hamm, Lucea, 18 April 1844, WMMS Jca., f2310.
47. D. King, *The State and Prospect of Jamaica* (Edinburgh 1850).
48. The Underhill letter to the Secretary of State for the Colonies, January 1865, presented BMS Secretary Underhill's observations supplemented by subsequent BMS missionary reports.
49. Tinson struggling to establish Calabar College made this point twice in 5 February – 12 March 1845, BMS Papers.
50. Knibb, Falmouth, 5 October 1844 and Clarke, Brown's Town, 20 July 1844, BMS Papers.
51. More fully discussed R. Stewart, *Religion and Society in Post-Emancipation Jamaica* (Knoxville: Univ. of Tennessee Press, 1992).
52. Jonathan Edmondson was chairman of the Jamaica District 1835-1865; he died in Jamaica in 1866.
53. Edmondson from Manchioneal and Duncans, 17 August 1849, and 19 November 1840, respectively, WMMS Jca., fs. 2339 and 2347.
54. Notable examples of active Jamaican missionaries in the 1840s and 1850s were John Vaz, Robert Johnson and Alexander Foote in the WMMS, Alexander Lindo in the LMS and of course the Moravian Archibald Monteith.
55. "Memorial of Ministers of all Denominations concerning the Evil of the Sugar Duties Act", chaired by R. Panton, Archdeacon of Surrey, with the Presbyterians, L. J. Watson, as secretary.
56. Wheeler, Kingston, 10 January 1851, LMS f605.
57. Stedman, Grateful Hill, 12 January 1852, WMMS Jca., f2348.
58. Hall, Kingston, 14 December 1852, LMS f612.
59. Holdsworth, Savanna-la-Mar, 10 July 1851, WMMS Jca., f2347.
60. Vaz, Port Antonio, 5 May 1852, WMMS Jca., f2350.
61. Hodgson, Yallahs, 19 August 1851, WMMS Jca., f2348.
62. Rowden, Lime Savanna, 23 December 1850, WMMS Jca., f2345.
63. Johnson, Spanish Town, 12 December 1850, WMMS Jca., f2345.
64. Young, Montego Bay, 9 December 1850, WMMS Jca., f2345.
65. Rev R. Panton's "Charges of corruption in the BMS in Jamaica", 1838. Panton was

Notes to pages 38–51

then corresponding secretary for the CMS. LMS Missionaries in Jamaica, "Baptist mission in Jamaica: an exposition of the system adopted by the Baptist missionaries in Jamaica", 1842 and a letter from the Presbyterian moderator, Peter Anderson, to BMS, 14 July 1841, printed as an Appendix in H.M. Waddell, *Twenty-Nine Years in the West Indies and Central Africa, 1829-1858* (London 1863).

66. Replies to Panton's charges by individual BMS missionaries, BMS Papers, 1839.
67. Reported by Millson, Mount Fletcher, 7 June 1864, WMMS Jca., f4392.
68. Gibson, Mandeville, 2 May 1840, LMS f553.
69. Barrett, Four Paths, 11 September 1840, LMS f3, f555.
70. See p 28 above.
71. Reported Tyson, Brown's Town, 21 July 1860, WMMS Jca, Box 199, f. 2371.
72. Covering letter with Memorial, Secretary Watson to all missionary societies and the Anti-Slavery Society requesting them to petition the British Parliament, 21 March 1852.
73. "Memorial of the Ministers".
74. "Memorial of the Ministers".
75. Report of the Stipendiary Magistrate, St Thomas-in-the-Vale, 1854.
76. Hornabrook, Kingston, 6 November 1845, WMMS Jca., f2319.

Chapter Three

1. Taylder, Montego Bay, 18 November 1844, WMMS Jca., f2313.
2. Thompson, Bath, 10 April 1845, WMMS Jca., f2315.
3. Dexter, Great River, 8 August 1840, BMS Papers. Dexter also promoted the free villages of Alps and Calabar in Trelawny.
4. Clarke, Brown's Town, 20 July 1844, BMS Papers.
5. Thompson, Wesley Mount, 4 January 1844, WMMS Jca., f2309.
6. Britten, Bath, 8 October 1847, WMMS Jca., f2330.
7. Edmondson, at Manchioneal, 17 August 1849, WMMS Jca., f2340.
8. Mary Knibb to Mrs Adey, Falmouth, 3 October 1837, BMS Papers.
9. Hornabrook, Mount Fletcher, 21 March 1849, WMMS Jca., f2338.
10. Edmondson, Kingston, 19 November 1849, WMMS Jca., f2342.
11. Edmondson, Kingston, 23 November 1863, WMMS Jca., f2388.
12. Memorial of Stewards and Members of Kingston Churches to explain "the serious declension in the income of the Society", forwarded by Bleby, 14 December 1846, WMMS Jca., f2324.
13. Tyson, Brown's Town, March 1858, WMMS Jca., f2363.
14. Gardner, Kingston, 23 March and 24 August 1865, LMS f659-660.
15. Alloway, Porus, 9 February 1855, LMS f624.
16. Resolutions of Morant Bay and Prospect LMS chapels, 21 September 1855, LMS f626.
17. Resolutions of Morant Bay and Prospect LMS chapels, July 1840, LMS f554.
18. Holland, Mount Zion, 24 March 1845, LMS f581.
19. Hillyer, Mount Zion, 8 February 1858, LMS f634.
20. Hornabrook, Kingston, 6 November 1845, WMMS Jca., f2319. Only the missionaries themselves contributed to the Fowell Buxton Memorial, at £2.10 a head.
21. *The Brethren's Church in Jamaica for the Past Hundred Years* (1854), MMS Papers.
22. Norman et al. Spanish Town, 7 August 1846, BMS Papers.
23. Clarke, *Memorials of Missionary Work in Jamaica* (1869).

Notes to pages 52–67

24. See p. 34 above.
25. Postscript to letter from J. MacLean and William James, trustees of Spanish Town Chapel, 17 April 1845, BMS Papers.
26. Thomas Robertson, trustee to Spanish Town Chapel, 19 April 1845, BMS Papers.
27. MacLean and James. See 25 above.
28. Robertson. See 26 above.
29. Minutes of half-yearly meeting, Clarendon LMS missionaries, 30 August 1843, LMS f472.
30. Minutes of subcommittee to examine the Mount Zion petition signed Barnett, 6 September 1843, LMS f573.
31. Hillyer, Mount Zion, 18 September 1843, LMS f573.
32. Hillyer, Mount Zion, 18 September 1843, LMS f573.
33. Jones reported the sequel, Mount Providence, 14 July 1844, LMS f576.
34. Deacons of Mount Zion, 6 September, 1852, LMS f612.
35. Gibson, Davyton, 8 October 1844, LMS f579.
36. Deacons of Davyton, 2 June 1850, LMS f603.
37. Lindo, Davyton, 9 August 1853, LMS f617.
38. Franklin, Morant Bay, 6 June 1845, LMS f581.
39. Franklin, Kingston, after his departure, 22 February 1847, LMS f588.
40. Members of Prospect Chapel, January 1851, LMS f605.
41. Deacons Robert White and William Bryan, Mandeville, 24 September 1854, LMS f623.
42. Foote was ordained at Bath 1848.
43. Vaz was ordained at Bath 1852.
44. Both ordained 1848.
45. Archibald Monteith's autobiography, 1853, in *Transactions of the Moravian Historical Society* 21 (1966): 46-48.
46. Foote, Manchioneal, 27 October 1846, WMMS Jca., f2325.
47. Vaz, Manchester, 26 January 1848, WMMS Jca., f2332.
48. Foote, Bath, 29 May 1850, WMMS Jca., f2344.
49. Lindo, Porus, 5 August 1857, LMS f632.
50. Lindo, Porus, 23 February 1864, LMS f655.
51. Edmondson, Kingston, 7 February 1863, WMMS Jca., f2384.
52. Edmondson, 18 June 1863, WMMS Jca., f2386.
53. Corlett, Montego Bay, 23 September 1864, WMMS Jca., f2392.
54. Fraser, St Ann's Bay, 7 July 1863, WMMS Jca., f2386.
55. Foote, Manchioneal, 7 July 1863, WMMS Jca., f2386.
56. Foote, Manchioneal, 28 April 1863, WMMS Jca., f2385.
57. Resolution of Kingston quarterly meeting, October 1864, WMMS Jca., f2392.
58. Foote, Manchioneal, 6 October 1864, WMMS Jca., f2392.
59. Geddes, Savanna-la-Mar, 7 October 1864, WMMS Jca., f2392.
60. Murray, Bath, 8 October 1864, WMMS Jca., f2392.
61. Peter Wilson, *Crab Antics* (New Haven: Yale Univ. Press, 1973).
62. Foote, Manchioneal, 7 June 1866, WMMS Jca., f2406.

Notes to pages 70–84

Chapter Four

1. Jamaica Royal Commission, 1866, Vol. 413, evidence of John McLaren.
2. JRC, Vol. 13, evidence of Minister Arthur Beckwith.
3. The Pennockites associated themselves with the British Methodist Free Church in 1864. At this point they had three native ministers, seven chapels and 1,100 members.
4. Woolridge, Kingston, 8 June 1835, LMS f525.
5. Atkin, Port Morant, 3 September 1844, WMMS Jca., f2312.
6. Thompson, Bath, 16 July 1845, WMMS Jca., f2316.
7. Johnson, Mandeville, 5 January 1846, WMMS Jca., f2320.
8. Edmondson, from Black River on tour, 3 November 1845, WMMS Jca., f2359.
9. Alloway, Dry Harbour, 19 May 1835, LMS f525.
10. Slayter, Porus, 16 June 1836, LMS f529.
11. Slayter, 23 February 1836, LMS f529.
12. Barrett, Four Paths, 30 March, 1836, LMS f530.
13. H. M Waddell, *Twenty-Nine Years in the West Indies and Central Africa, 1829-1858* (London 1863), 111.
14. Quoted schoolmaster, Brown, Mandeville, 3 October 1836, LMS f534.
15. Conversation reported (Franklin, Morant Bay), 2 October 1839, LMS f550.
16. Reported by Sedden to CMS, quoted *Church Missionary Record* 4 (1834).
17. See p. 55 above.
18. See p. 70 above, for example.
19. See pp. 38-39 above.
20. An Accompong woman to CMS missionary Gillies, quoted *Church Missionary Record* 10 (1839).
21. Woolridge, Kingston, 12 March 1838, LMS f540.
22. Woolridge, Kingston, 12 March 1838, LMS f540.
23. Reported by Holland, Mount Regale, 26 July 1843, LMS f572.
24. Quoted by Gibson, Ridgemount, 2 May 1840, LMS f553.
25. Sam Oughton's Baptism Book, n.d., BMS papers.
26. Schoolmaster Milne, Mount Regale, February 1840, LMS f572.
27. Holland, Mount Regale, 7 July 1842, LMS f512.
28. Holland, 26 July 1843, LMS f572.
29. See pp. 54-56 above.
30. "Minutes of the subcommittee to examine petitions from the Mount Regale members", 6 September 1843, LMS f573.
31. Alloway, Porus, 21 July 1846, LMS f585.
32. Franklin, Morant Bay, 21 July 1840, LMS f554.
33. Wilkinson, Kingston, 15 November 1842, LMS f569.
34. Waddell, *Twenty-Nine Years*, 191.
35. Waddell, *Twenty-Nine Years*, 193.
36. M. Schuler, *Alas, Alas, Kongo* (Baltimore: Johns Hopkins Univ. Press, 1980) and M. Alleyne, *Roots of Jamaican Culture* (London: Pluto Press, 1988).
37. Well discussed by Garnet Roper, "The impact of evangelical and pentecostal religion", *Caribbean Quarterly* 37, no. 1 (March 1991).

Notes to pages 86–100

Chapter Five

1. Tyson, Brown's Town, 23 April 1861, WMMS Jca., f2375.
2. Raspass, Savanna-la-Mar, 6 May 1861, WMMS Jca.,f2375.
3. Foote, Manchioneal, 8 July 1861, WMMS Jca., f2376.
4. Foote, Manchioneal, 8 July 1861, WMMS Jca., f2376.
5. Alloway, Ridgemount, 6 November 1860, LMS f645.
6. Fletcher, Chapelton, 19 February 1861, LMS f646.
7. Buchner quoted in MMS, *The Breaking of the Dawn* (1904).
8. Corlett, Montego Bay, 8 December 1860, WMMS Jca., f2372.
9. Holdsworth, Guys Hill, 6 May 1861, WMMS Jca., f2375.
10. Hillyer, Mount Zion, 7 January 1861, LMS f646.
11. Haine, Duncans, 28 January 1861, WMMS Jca., f2373.
12. Foote, Manchioneal, 22 April 1861, WMMS Jca., f2374.
13. Edman, Yallahs, 24 October 1861, WMMS Jca., f2378.
14. Holdsworth, Guys Hill, 7 March 1861, WMMS Jca., f2373.
15. Holdsworth, Guys Hill, 23 October 1861, WMMS Jca., f2378.
16. Geddes, Port Royal, 22 April 1861, WMMS Jca., f2374.
17. Atkinson, Linstead, 7 October 1861, WMMS Jca., f2378.
18. Resolution of LMS missionaries, Kingston, 7 February 1861, LMS f646.
19. It is noteworthy that most of the St Thomas-in-the-East native Baptist women who gave evidence to the 1866 JRC said they were married and concerned with the fate of their husbands during martial law.

Chapter Six

1. US Consular Despatch, 8 January 1839, reel 6.
2. US Consular Despatch, 17 October 1834, warns that Knibb and Burchell have been instructed by the British Anti-Slavery Society to campaign in the Southern States. A despatch of 23 October 1835 warns of a few dissenting missionaries travelling to US with copies of the *Watchman*; 10 January 1837 warns that the *West Indian* is "intended for circulation in the US", reel 5.
3. US Consular Despatch, 3 April 1836, reel 4.
4. US Consular Despatch, 27 July and 15 November 1847, reel 10.
5. US Consular Despatch, 14 February 1851, reel 13.
6. US Consular Despatch, 24 April 1853, reel 14.
7. US Consular Despatch, 17 July 1855, reel 17.
8. US Consular Despatch, 10 October 1855, reel 17.
9. Quoted, but not discussed, R. Stewart, *Religion and Society in Post-Emancipation Jamaica* (Knoxville: Univ. of Tennessee Press, 1992), 121.
10. Secretary of BMS, Underhill, to Secretary of State, Cardwell, London, 5 January 1865. Distributed to custodes, magistrates and ministers of all churches by Governor Eyre, March 1865. Published *Jamaica Guardian*, 21 March 1865.
11. Gordon at Underhill meetings in St Ann and St Thomas-in-the-East quoted Ansell Hart, *The Life of George William Gordon* (Kingston: Institute of Jamaica, 1975), 65-66.
12. E.B. Underhill, *The Tragedy of Morant Bay* (London 1895).

Notes to pages 101–117

13. Petition to the Queen of "The poor people of St Ann's Parish", May 1864, signed by 108 petitioners, 82 by an X. Quoted in S. Gordon, *Caribbean Generations* (London: Longman, 1983), 203-4.
14. Ministers of the JBU to the Governor, May 1865, BMS Papers.
15. Edmondson to Colonial Secretary, Kingston, 20 April 1865, in response to Underhill Letter, WMMS Jca., f2396.
16. Gardner to Governor Eyre, Kingston, 24 October 1865, LMS f661.
17. Selected resolutions from Underhill meetings quoted Gordon, *Caribbean Generations*, 202, 205.
18. Petition to the Governor from Paul Bogle and others, Stony Gut, 10 October 1865, quoted Gordon, *Caribbean Generations*, 205-6.
19. Gordon to Bogle, Kingston, 5 February 1864, Report of JRC, Vol. 4, 1866, "The case of George William Gordon".
20. Report of JRC, Vol. 4, 1866, "The case of George William Gordon".
21. Gordon to Bogle, Report of JRC, Vol. 4, 1866, "The case of George William Gordon".
22. Many witnesses to the JRC said that they had been required to take an oath on the Bible in their meeting houses promising support for Paul Bogle's protest before travelling to Stony Gut to find out what was expected of them. E.g. Osborne and Jacob, JRC, Vol. 412; Botawell, Gordon, Onslow, Moody, Mclara, JRC, Vol. 413.
23. Ross quoted by Gardner, Kingston, 7 January 1865, LMS f659.
24. Joyce, Mount Zion, 4 November 1865, LMS f661.
25. Whitehouse, St Ann's Bay, 3 March 1866, WMMS Jca., f2404. He was responding to a warning from the London Committee to avoid such comments while the JRC was sitting.
26. Alloway, Mandeville, 23 October 1865, LMS f661.
27. Milne, First Hill, 6 November 1865, LMS f661.
28. Clark, Four Paths, 23 October 1865, LMS f661.
29. Gardner, Kingston, 24 October 1865, LMS f661.
30. Edmondson, Kingston, 23 October 1865, WMMS Jca., f2401.
31. Gardner, Kingston, 9 December 1865, LMS f662.
32. Mearns, Montego Bay, May 1865, WMMS Jca., f2397.
33. Mearns, 23 October 1865, WMMS Jca., f2401.
34. Mearns, 23 December, 1865, WMMS Jca., f2403.
35. Lindo, Porus, 6 January 1866, LMS f662.
36. Parnther, Morant Bay, 21 October 1865, WMMS Jca., f2401.
37. Parnther reported through Edmondson, Kingston, 23 October 1865, WMMS Jca., f2401.
38. Parnther, 20 December 1865, WMMS Jca., f2403.
39. Foote, Manchioneal, 23 November 1865, WMMS Jca., f2402.
40. Harty, Prospect, 22 November 1865, LMS f661.
41. Harty, 13 January 1866, LMS f663.
42. Harty, 20 September 1866, LMS f664.
43. Murray, Bath, 25 October 1865, WMMS Jca., f2401.
44. Murray, 23 December, 1866, WMMS Jca., f2403.
45. Murray, 23 December, 1866, WMMS Jca., f2403.
46. "The report of the religious state of Bath", forwarded with comment by Mearns to WMMS, 23 December 1865, WMMS Jca., f2403.
47. Mearns to WMMS, Kingston, 6 January 1866, enclosing a copy of the memorial

from the ministers of the three dissenting chapels in Montego Bay, WMMS Jca., f2404.
48. Mearns, 6 April 1866, WMMS Jca., f2405.
49. East to the Secretary of State for the Colonies, Calabar College, 6 January 1866, BMS Papers.

Conclusion

1. Homi Bhabha, *The Location of Culture* (London: Routledge, 1994), 89.
2. P. Curtin, *The Two Jamaicas* (1955; reprint New York: Greenwood Press, 1968), 208.
3. Noel Erskine, *Decolonizing Theology: A Caribbean Perspective* (Mary Knoll, NY: Orbis Books, 1981), 100-101.
4. Robert Stewart, *Religion and Society in Post Emancipation Jamaica* (Knoxville: University of Tennessee Press, 1992), 96-106, gives an account of Rev Robert Gordon's career.
5. See above pp. 79-82.
6. Quoted Erskine, *Decolonizing Theology*, 100.
7. Erskine, *Decolonizing Theology*, 106.
8. JRC, 1866, Vol. 417, Evidence of Alexander Lothwell of Spring Gardens, Francis Gordon and William Onslow of Stanton, John Moody of Monklands, J. McLaren of Fonthill and George Lake of Torrington.
9. JRC, Vol. 417, evidence of George Fuller Osborne, leader of the police group sent to Stony Gut, confirmed by policemen, William Lake, Charles Jacob and James Foster who said they took the oath in a language they could not understand.
10. JRC, Vol. 417, letter produced by Gordon Ramsay, and addressed to "Mr Graham and other gentlemen" from P. Bogle, J.G. McLaren, B. Clarke and P. Cameron.
11. Amy Jaques-Garvey (ed.), *Philosophy and Opinions of Marcus Garvey*, vol. 1 (New York: Atheneum, 1969), 62.

Bibliography

Manuscript Sources

Baptist Missionary Society

Missionary Correspondence WI/1-5, 1837-65
Autobiography of J.M. Phillippo, n.d., WI/1
Fenn Collection, including correspondence between J. Sturge and J. Clark, 1837-58
Sam Oughton's Baptism Book, n.d.
Letters from J. Angus on visit to Jamaica, 1846-47, including papers on the Spanish Town dispute. H11 3/4

London Missionary Society

West Indies–Jamaica Correspondence in the School of African and Oriental Studies
    Fiche boxes 13-16
    13: 1830-43
    14: 1843-53
    15: 1853-65
    16: 1865-67

Moravian Missionary Society

Minutes of the Society for the Furtherance of the Gospel (London association of MMS) VI-VIII, 1839-69

Wesleyan Methodist Missionary Society in the School of African and Oriental Studies

Missionary Correspondence
    West Indies fiche boxes
    133: 1833
    134: Jan-Jun 1834
    135: Jul-Dec 1835
    136: Jan-Jun 1835

137: Jul-Dec 1835
138: 1836
139: 1837
139: 1837
140: 1838-42

Jamaica fiche boxes
47: 1833-39
48: 1840-44
49: 1848
50: 1866-72

Public Record Office, UK

Colonial Office Records:
Governors' Despatches, 1838-65, CO 137
Ecclesiastical Correspondence, CO 137, 272 & 299
Report of Jamaica Royal Commission, 1866, CO 137, 411-20

British Library: Humanities and Social Sciences

United States Consular Despatches, Kingston
Microfilm reels 4-22, 1835-65

Printed Primary Sources

Missionary

Accounts of the Baptist Missionary Society, 1837-39
Baptist Herald, 1839-46
Church Missionary Record
Periodical Accounts of the Moravian Missionary Society, 1836-65
Annual Reports of the Wesleyan Methodist Missionary Society, 1836-65

Newspapers

Falmouth Post
Jamaica Standard and Royal Gazette
Jamaica Watchman & People's Free Press
Morning Journal

Parliamentary Papers

1841 111 (344) Papers Relative to the West Indies, Part II, Jamaica
1842 XXIX (374) Papers Relative to the West Indies, 1841-42, Jamaica

Bibliography

Selected Secondary Sources

Contemporary and Church/Mission Related

Bleby, Henry. 1853. *Death Struggles of Slavery*. London.
Blyth, George. 1853. *Reminiscences of a Missionary Life*. London.
Buchner, John. 1854. *The Moravians in Jamaica*. London.
Burchell, William. 1849. *Memoir of Thomas Burchell*. London.
Caldecott, Alfred. 1898. *The Church in the West Indies*. London.
Clarke, John. 1869. *Memorials of Baptist Missionaries in Jamaica*. London.
Clarke, John, Walter Dendy, and James Phillippo. 1865. *The Voice of Jubilee*. London.
Duncan, Peter. 1849. *A Narrative of the Wesleyan Mission to Jamaica*. London.
Ellis, John. 1913. *The Diocese of Jamaica*. London: SPCK.
Findlay, George, and William Holdsworth. 1924. *The History of the Wesleyan Missionary Society*. London: Epworth Press.
Gardner, William. 1873. *A History of Jamaica*. London.
Harvey, Thomas, and William Brewin. 1867. *Jamaica in 1866*. London.
Hinton, John. 1847. *Memoir of William Knibb*. London.
King, David. 1850. *The State and Prospect of Jamaica*. Edinburgh.
Lovett, Richard. 1899. *History of the London Missionary Society, 1795-1895*. London.
Moravian Missionary Society. 1854. *The Brethren's Church in Jamaica for the Past Hundred Years*. London.
Phillippo, James. 1843. *Jamaica: Its Past and Present State*. London.
Sewell, William. 1861. *The Ordeal of Free Labor in the West Indies*. Reprint, 1968. London: Frank Cass.
Sturge, Joseph, & Thomas Harvey. 1838. *The West Indies in 1837*. London.
Tucker, Leonard. 1914. *Glorious Liberty, the Story of a Hundred Years? Work of the Jamaica Baptist Mission*. London.
Underhill, Edward. 1862. *The West Indies, Their Social and Religious Condition*. London.
Underhill, Edward. 1879. *Life of James Mursell Phillippo, Missionary in Jamaica*. London.
Underhill, Edward. 1895. *The Tragedy of Morant Bay*. London.
Waddell, Hope Masterton. 1863. *Twenty-Nine Years in the West Indies and Central Africa, 1829-1858*. London.

Related Themes

Alleyne, Mervyn. 1988. *Roots of Jamaican Culture*. London: Pluto Press.
Aptheker, Herbert. 1951. *A Documentary History of the Negro People in the United States*. Reprint, 1990. Secaucus: Citadel Press.
Bastide, Roger. 1967. *African Civilisations in the New World*. Trans., Baltimore: Johns Hopkins University Press.
Beckwith, Martha. 1919. *Black Roadways*. Reprint, 1929. New York: Negro University Press.
Beidelman, T.O. 1989. *Colonial Evangelism*. Bloomington: Indiana University Press.
Bhabha, Homi, 1994. *The Location of Culture*. London & New York: Routledge.
Birkett, Randall. 1978. *Garveyism as a Religious Movement*. New York: Scarecrow Press.
Bisnauth, Dale. 1989. *History of Religions in the Caribbean*. Kingston: Kingston Publishers.

Bibliography

Blackburn, Robin. 1988. *The Overthrow of Colonial Slavery*. London: Verso.
Boles, John B., ed. 1988. *Masters and Slaves in the House of the Lord: Race and Religion in the American South 1740-1870*. Lexington: University of Kentucky Press.
Bryan, Patrick. 1991. *The Jamaican People, 1880-1902*. London: Macmillan.
Burn, William. 1937. *Emancipation and Apprenticeship in the British West Indies*. London: Jonathan Cape.
Campbell, Mavis. 1976. *The Dynamics of Change in a Slave Society, 1800-65*. London: Associated Universities Press.
Chevannes, Barry (ed.). 1995. *Rastafari and other African-Caribbean World Views*. London: Macmillan.
Cooper, Carolyn. 1993. *Noises in the Blood*. London: Macmillan.
Crahan, Margaret, and Franklin Knight, eds. 1979. *Africa and the Caribbean: the Legacies of a Link*. Baltimore: Johns Hopkins University Press.
Curtin, Philip. 1972. *Africa and the West*. Madison: University of Wisconsin Press.
Curtin, Philip. 1955. *The Two Jamaicas*. Reprint, 1968, New York: Greenwood Press.
Durkheim, Emile. 1915. *The Elementary Forms of the Religious Life*. Reprint, 1971. London: Allen & Unwin.
Eisner, Gisela. 1961. *Jamaica, 1830-1930*. Manchester: Manchester University Press.
Erskine, Noel. 1981. *Decolonizing Theology: a Caribbean Perspective*. Mary Knoll, New York: Orbis.
Fanon, Frantz. 1952. *Black Skin White Masks*. Trans., Reprint, 1967. New York: Grove Press.
Garvey, Amy Jacques (ed.). 1969. *Philosophy and Opinions of Marcus Garvey*. New York: Atheneum.
Genovese, Eugene. 1974. *Roll, Jordan, Roll: the World the Slaves Made*. New York: Pantheon Books.
Gordon, Shirley C. 1996. *God Almighty Make Me Free: Christianity in Preemancipation Jamaica*. Bloomington: University of Indiana Press.
Green, William. 1976. *British Slave Emancipation, 1830-65*. Oxford: Clarendon Press.
Hall, Douglas. [1959] 1969. *Free Jamaica, 1836-65*. Barbados: Caribbean Universities Press.
Hart, Ansell. 1972. *Life of George William Gordon*. Kingston: Institute of Jamaica.
Herskovitz, Melville. 1941. *The Myth of the Negro Past*. Reprint, 1958. Boston: Beacon Press.
Heuman, Gad. 1981. *Black and White: Race, Politics and the Free Coloureds in Jamaica, 1792-1865*. Oxford: Clio Press.
Heuman, Gad. 1994. *The Killing Time: the Morant Bay Rebellion in Jamaica*. London: Macmillan.
Holt, Thomas. 1992. *The Problem of Freedom: Race, Labor and Politics in Jamaica and Britain, 1832-1838*. Baltimore: John Hopkins University Press.
Jacobs, H.P. 1973. *Sixty Years of Change*. Kingston: Institute of Jamaica.
Knight, Franklin, and Peggy K. Liss. 1991. *Atlantic Port Cities 1650-1850*. Knoxville, University of Tennessee Press.
Kolchin, Peter. 1993. *American Slavery, 1619-1877*. Toronto: HarperCollins.
Laguerre, Michael. 1989. *Voodoo and Politics in Haiti*. London: Macmillan.
Latimer, James. 1984. *Foundations of the Christian Missions in the British, French and Spanish West Indies*. New York: Vantage Press.
Lawson, Winston. 1996. *Religion and Race: African and European Roots in Conflict – A Jamaican Testament*. New York: Peter Lang.

Bibliography

Lewis, Gordon. 1983. *Main Currents in Caribbean Thought*. London: Heinemann.
Lewis, Rupert. 1987. *Marcus Garvey: Colonial Champion*. London: Karia Press.
Mathieson, William. 1932. *British Slave Emancipation, 1838-45*. London.
Mintz, Sidney. 1974. *Caribbean Transformations*. Chicago: Aldine Press.
Mintz, Sidney, and Richard Price. 1976. *An Anthropological Approach to the African Past: a Caribbean Perspective*. Philadelphia: Institute for the Study of Human Issues.
McLewin, Philip. 1987. *Power and Economic Change*. London & New York: Garland.
Mullin, Michael. 1992. *Africa in America: Slave Acculturation and Resistance in the American South and British Caribbean, 1736-1831*. Chicago: University of Illinois Press.
Nettleford, Rex. 1970. *Mirror, Mirror, Identity, Race and Protest*. Glasgow: Collins/Sangster.
Nettleford, Rex. 1978. *Cultural Identity: the Case of Jamaica*. Kingston: Institute of Jamaica.
Nettleford, Rex. 1993. *Inward Stretch, Outward Reach: A Voice from the Caribbean*. London: Macmillan.
Nicholls, David. 1988. *Dessalines to Duvalier*. London: Macmillan.
Oliver, Roland. 1991. *The African Experience*. London: Weidenfeld & Nicholson.
Osborne, Francis. 1977. *History of the Catholic Church in Jamaica*. Reprint, 1988. Chicago: Loyola Press.
Owens, Joseph. 1977. *Dread: The Rastafarians of Jamaica*. Kingston: Sangster.
Ownby, Ted. 1993. *Black and White: Cultural Interaction in the Antibellum South*. Jackson: University of Mississippi Press.
Raboteau, Albert. 1978. *Slave Religion*. New York: Oxford University Press.
Robotham, Don. 1981. *The Notorious Riot: the Socio-Economic and Political Bases of Paul Bogle's Revolt*. Working Paper No. 28. Kingston: Institute of Social & Economic Research, University of the West Indies.
Said, Edward. 1994. *Culture and Imperialism*. London: Vintage.
Schuler, Monica. 1980. *Alas, Alas, Kongo: A Social History of Indentured African Immigration into Jamaica 1841-1865*. Baltimore: Johns Hopkins University Press.
Sibley, Inez. 1965. *Baptists of Jamaica*. Kingston: Jamaica Baptist Union.
Simpson, George. 1978. *Black Religions in the New World*. New York: Columbia University Press.
Simpson, George. 1970. *Religious Cults in the Caribbean: Jamaica, Trinidad and Haiti*. Puerto Rico: Institute of Caribbean Studies.
Smith, M.G., R. Augier, and R. Nettleford. 1960. *The Rastafari Movement in Kingston, Jamaica*. Kingston: Institute of Social and Economic Research, University College of the West Indies.
Stewart, Robert, *Religion and Society in Post-Emancipation Jamaica*, 1992, Knoxville: University of Tennessee Press.
Stuckey, Sterling. 1987. *Slave Culture: Nationalist Theory and the Foundations of Black America*, New York: Oxford University Press.
Turner, Mary. 1982. *Slaves and Missionaries: The Disintegration of Jamaican Slave Society 1787-1834*. Urbana: University of Illinois Press.
Turner, Mary, (ed.) 1995. *From Chattel Slaves to Wage Slaves: the Dynamics of Slave Bargaining in the Americas*. Kingston, Bloomington & London: Ian Randle, Indiana University Press & James Currey.
University of the West Indies, Department of History. 1980. *Jamaica Censuses*. Kingston: Department of History, University of the West Indies.

Bibliography

Wilson, Peter. 1972. *Crab Antics*. New Haven: Yale University Press.
Wood, Betty. 1995. *Women's Work, Men's Work: the Informal Slave Economies of Low-country Georgia*. Athens: University of Georgia Press.

Articles

Besson, Jean. 1987. "Family land as a model for Martha Brae's new history: culture building in an Afro-Caribbean village". *African-Caribbean Institute of Jamaica Research Review*, no. 2.
Brathwaite, E. Kamau. 1978. "Kumina: the spirit of African survival". *Jamaica Journal* 42 (September).
Bryan, Patrick. 1986. "Archbishop Nuttall and the survival of the 'White Man's Church' in Jamaica". *Jamaican Historical Review* 15.
Campbell, Carl. 1970. "Social and economic obstacles to the development of popular education in post-emancipation Jamaica". *Journal of Caribbean History* 1.
Chevannes, Barry. 1971. "Revival and black struggle". *Savacou* 5.
Chevannes, Barry. 1991. "Towards an Afro-Caribbean theology". *Caribbean Quarterly* 37, no. 1 (March).
Crahan, Margaret, and Franklin Knight. 1979. "The African migration". In *Africa and the Caribbean: the Legacies of a Link*, edited by M. Crahan & F. Knight. Baltimore: Johns Hopkins University Press.
Lewis, Maureen Warner. 1977. "The Nkuyu: spirit messengers of the Kumina". *Savacou* 13.
Mintz, Sidney. 1987. "The historical sociology of Jamaican villages". *African-Caribbean Institute of Jamaica Research Review*, no 2.
Russell, Horace. 1983. "The church in the past: a study on Jamaican Baptists in the 18th and 19th centuries". *Jamaican Historical Society Bulletin* 8.
Russell, Horace. 1983. "The emergence of the Christian black: the making of a stereotype". *Jamaica Journal* 16, no. 1 (February).
Roper, Garnet. 1991. "The impact of evangelical and pentecostal religion". *Caribbean Quarterly* 37, no. 1 (March).
Schuler, Monica. 1979. "Myalism and the African religious tradition in Jamaica". In *Africa and the Caribbean: the Legacies of a Link*, edited by M. Crahan and F. Knight. Baltimore: Johns Hopkins University Press.
Seaga, Edward. 1969. "Revival cults in Jamaica". *Jamaica Journal* 3, no. 2.
Stewart, Robert. 1993. "A slandered people: views on "Negro Character? in the mainstream Christian churches in postemancipation Jamaica". Paper presented at the Association of Caribbean Historians Conference, UWI Mona, Jamaica, April.
Taylor, Burchell. 1991. "The theology of liberation". *Caribbean Quarterly* 37, No. 1 (March).
Wilmot, Swithin. 1983. "Sugar and the Gospel: Baptist perspectives on the plantation in the early period of freedom". *Jamaican Historical Society Bulletin* 8.
Wilmot, Swithin. 1985. "From Falmouth to Morant Bay: religion and politics in Jamaica 1838-65". Paper presented at the Association of Caribbean Historians Conference, Havana, April.
Wilmot, Swithin. 1990. "Politics of protest in free Jamaica". *Caribbean Quarterly* 36 (December).

Bibliography

Theses

Catherall, Gordon. 1966. "The Baptist Missionary Society and Jamaican emancipation". MA thesis, University of Liverpool.

Ryall, Dorothy. 1959. "The organization of the missionary societies, the recruitment of the missionaries in Britain and the role of the missionaries in the diffusion of British culture in Jamaica during the period 1834-65". PhD diss., University of London.

Williams, Fay. 1987. "The work of the Anglican church in education in Jamaica, 1826-45". MA thesis, University of the West Indies.

Wilmot, Swithin. 1977. "Political developments in Jamaica in the postemancipation period, 1838-54". PhD diss., Oxford University.

Index

Abolition of slavery: British, viii, xiii, 5, 11, 25; American, 5, 6, 99

Africa: return to on death, xiv; back to, 25; focus of Jamaican missionary effort, 50, 51, 60, 77, 78; migrants from, 83-84; as home land, 121

African religious beliefs: life after death, vii; imported by slaves, xiv, 121; imported by immigrants, 83-84; spirit-centred, 84; cleansing powers of water, 84; hierarchy of office holders, 84; secret oaths, 124

Afro-Jamaican Christianity: syncretic with African survivals, ix, 3; in uncoordinated groups, ix, 3, 69, 121; in variety of popular local versions, x, 2, 3, 69, 73; Jamaican initiatives in: xvi, 2, 3, 74, 125; parallel development with missions, xvii, 2, 71, 82; despised as heathen by missionaries: 37, 75, 78, 84; ecstatic participation in worship, 2, 3, 68, 84, 120, 123; support for deprived, 9, 121; community organisation, 9, 123; growing following for: 69, 93, 120; expressed in Great Revival, 86, 88, 93, 120; this worldly concerns, 107-108, 119, 12; black leadership in, 120; accepting common law partners, 121. *See also* Independent religious groups and Native Baptists.

Afro-Jamaican religion: syncretic African and native Baptist, ix, x, 84; spirit worship, x, 3, 4, 7, 74, 75, 76; superstition and heathenism to missionaries, x, 84, 87, 88; black leadership, x, xi, 84, 121; adoption from mission Christianity, 76, 85, 120; new rituals introduced by African immigrants, 83-84. *See also* Myal and Obeah

American blacks: arrivals, 6, 97-99; popular support for, 97, 98; freed in Jamaica, 97-99

Anti-slavery activities: in Britain, ix, xv, 36, 41, 97, 134 fn2; in USA, ix, 6, 97, in Jamaica, 97-99

Apprenticeship: missionary heyday 10-13 passim; missionary support for apprentices, 1, 11, 12; exploitation of, 11; apprentices' thirst for literacy, 13, 16

Aspirations: for freedom, ix, xvi, 27; for literacy, ix, 5, 12, 13, 14; for free life style, 1, 2; for recognition in free society, xvi, 10, 12, 68; to emigrate, 18; for education, 22, 24, 25; declining, 32, 70; for Jamaican identity, 96, 97, 105. *See also* Social Mobility and Status

Baker, Moses (Black American Baptist): 4, 74

Baptism: in missions, 27, 29, 38, 45, 79; in native religious groups, 71, 74, 84, 94; ensuring salvation, 76-77, 79

Baptist Missionary Society (BMS): political parsons, 12; need for native pastors recognised, 19, 59, 63; Calabar training school, 19, 51, 63; free villages, 26, 29, 39, 54; stations, 26, 30, 38, 39, 40; declining influence, 29, 33, 54; home society, 32, 38-39; Spanish Town chapel dispute, 33-34, 52-54 passim; charges against by other missions, 38-39, 75; schools, 39; relations with native Baptists, 39, 82; Jamaican missionaries to W. Africa, 51-52; missionaries declare financial independence, 63; promote Underhill visit, 100

BMS missionaries: T. Burchell, 12, 30; B. Dexter 47, 131 fn3; F. Gardner; 71, 77; J. Iisnon, 71; S. Oughton, 79; E. Palmer (Jamaican), 109; J. Clark, 40, 47, 51. *See also* William Knibb

Bazaars: 47, 48

Index

Beckwith, Arthur (Independent preacher): 2, 69, 70, 104, 105

Bible: language of, xvii, 59, 76, 122; Native Baptist attitudes to, 74-75, 107, 124; as religious guide, xvii, 78, 121

Black American Baptists: arrival, viii, xiii, 4, 5, intelligence of, 5; contemptuous of white missionaries, 5; abiding influence of 94, 99. See also Moses Baker and George Liele

Black awareness: solidarity through, xi, 80, 99, 124; with landed American slaves, 6, 97-98, 99, 121

Bogle Paul: calls for black solidarity, xi, 99, 124, 125; mobilises followers, 5, 105, 110, 125; petitions for land access, 101, 104-105; relations with G. W. Gordon, 106; reward for capture, 109

British citizenship: ex-slaves, 2, 11; of missionaries, 11, 60; of Jamaicans, 53, 60, 105, 119, 122

British Government: backs religious bodies for ex-slaves instruction, ix, 11, 120; Negro Education Grant, 3, 13; Sugar Duties Act, 3, 36; thanked for boon of freedom, 10, 32; disestablishment of colonial Anglican churches 58, 146, 172

British missionary societies: metropolitan connections of British missionaries, x; missionary correspondence with: x, xvi, 4, 10, 52, 29, 36, 93; address by Jamaican laity, xvi, 20, 33-34, 48, 52-56; embargo on socio-political comment, 2, 4, 9, 21; assistance with chapel costs, 27, 39; overextended, 32, 59; urging self sufficiency/native pastors, 32, 59, 62-63; disputed ownership of chapels, 32, 33, 72; missionary appeals to for resources, 32, 36, 48, 93; lay appeals to for continued support, 32, 59; disowning chapel debts, 46. See also individual missions

Buchner, John: (MMS) 18, 28, 90

Censuses: 26, 29, fn4

Chapels: missionary, viii, x, xiii, 26, 32-33, 46, 48, 53, 72, 85; built by members, 27, 28, 33, 46, 47; on British models, 27, 33; in free villages, 27, 28; debts, 32, 33; Native Baptist & Independent, 40, 70, 72, 81, 103, 107; used in Great Revival, 86, 87

Children: manumitted, ix; ex-slave, ix, xvi, 12, 85; school, 5, 12, 14, 16,17; working, 15; illegitimate, 101. See also Youth/juveniles

Christian doctrine/teaching: pronounced in sermons, xiii, xiv, 79; mainly learnt from leaders, viii, xiv, 33, 45, 77; life after death, xiv, xv, 79; all equal in eyes of God, xiv; limited understanding of, 15, 16; lay discussion of, 77, 78; atonement, 79; salvation, 79, 84; divine judgement, 79-80; divine mercy, 79-80; Jamaican discussion of, 77, 78

Church Missionary Society (CMS): 19, 75, 128, fn2

Class: fledgling middle, 7, 25, 67, 68, 120; labouring, 11, 12, 36, 120; appropriate education for, 113, 18; growing middle class, 96, 121, 122, 124

Clerks, sales people, storekeepers: 2, 96

Clothes: Sunday unaffordable, 3, 29, 32, 102, 103; status symbol, 107, 112; school, 10, 25

Colonial authorities (establishment, government): little concerned with religious life, 2; unwilling to provide schools, 15; alarmed by native Baptist groups, 100, 107. See also Governors and House of Assembly

Crown Colony Government: 67, 114, 121, 124

Colonial Church Union: 11, 33, 128, fn3

Colour: class factor, 28, 99; allegations of prejudice in Methodist mission, 33-34; an issue in Morant Bay protest, 108, 109, 110

Coloured people: in chapels, 14, 48; claim status, 64-65; native missionaries, 64

Congregationalists (American): 6, 40

Crops: food and town market 12, 46, 92; diversified for export, 96, 101, 122. See also Sugar production

Conversion: not to be completed by missions, 3, 4, 29, 30, 34, 120; leaders bedrock of, 4, 33, 45; education seen as best means, 2, 13-26 passim; varied interpretations of, 30, 76-77, 79; replaced as purpose by static ministries, 43-44; in Great Revival, 92-93

Convince: 76, 78, 84. See also Spirits

Crime: result of failure in sugar, 43; in city, 43; praedial larceny, 43, 103; attributed to native Baptists, 80, 108; juvenile, 101, 102

145

Index

Deacons: *See* Leaders

Denominationalism: not a Jamaican concern, 2, 31, 70, 122; missionary rivalry, 38-39, 40, 122

Disputes: over chapels 7, 33, 34, 48, 53, 72; Spanish Town BMS, 33-34, 52-54; Mount Zion LMS, 54-56; Morant Bay LMS, 57-58

Dawson, Thomas (BMS/Indep. Baptist), 34, 53, 71

Dreams (visions): qualification for baptism, 184; in Great Revival, 92; of the millenium, 121; mentioned, 34, 53, 71

Dual membership: *See* Transfers of allegiance

Dual development of Christianity: wide differences, xvii, 9; counterpoint pattern of, 121, 126; related to socioeconomic experience, 123-124

Eastwood, James (Jamaican LMS assistant missionary): 17, 22, 129 fn 13

Edmondson Jonathan (WMMS Chairman): favourism ministerial training in Jamaica, 24, 64; on missionary losses, 35; critical of Puseyism in Established Church, 39; on chapel increases, 47, 48; against lower salaries for Jamaican missionaries, 64; recognises native Baptists as equal rivals with Established Church, 72; on Underhill Letter, 102-103; on Morant Bay Riot, 109-110

Education: religious, 2, 13-26 passim; missionary purpose for, 6, 9, 13, 39; consumers' purpose for, 2, 5, 12, 14, 16, 18; elementary criticised, 18-19; need for secondary/high schools, 23, 25, 68, 122; divisive effect of, 25; agricul- tural suggested, 103. *See also* Schooling

Emancipation: Baptist War as Instrumental to, ix; a stage in Jamaican Christianity, ix, 1; missionary heyday following, 2, 10-13 passim; annual thanksgivings for, 10; dying euphoria after, 42, 43, 85

Employment: decline in, ix, 1, 3, 27, 31, 32, away from home, 18; lack of 18, 104

Epidemics: 3, 37-38

Established Church: Anglican see, xiii; expanding missionary activities, 10, 31; lenient to immorality, 31, 39; supported by Colonial Government, 31, 39; no dues or fees, 31, 39; attracting defectors from missions, 39, 48; stations, 40; rectors, 40, 109; Disestablishment of, 39, 67, 96, 103, 121; attracts middle class membership, 96, 12

Euro-Christianity: promoted in missions, ix-x, 120; modern search for Jamaican version, xi, 124; parallel development with Afro-Christianity, xvii, 9, 121, 126; European social and moral values, 67, 120, 121; model for middle class living, 68; white man's Christianity, 77; widening gulf with Afro-Christian religion, 9, 82; disapproval of popular protest, 107-108

European missions: in slavery, viii, ix; dependence on leaders, deacons etc., viii, 9, 33, 45, 76, 77; arena for free black and coloured influenced, viii, x, xiii, xv, 11; islandwide orgnisation, x; metropolitan organisation, x, xvi, 13, 22; chapel stewards, ix, xvi, 28, 41; dues, fees, collections, 3, 4, 7, 36, 50; elementary schooling 13-15 passim, 17-19 passim, 20, 25; Sunday (Sabbath) schools, 2, 4, 9, 13, 74; training schools, 20-21; mission property, 26, 27, 31; system of churches and schools founded, 120. *See also* BMS, CMS, MMS, WMMS

European missionaries: *See* Afro-Jamaican religion as heathenism, ix, 75, 78, 84; deny Christianity of independent religious groups, x, 37, 81, 84; ambivalence about Great Revival, x, 7, 86, 87, 88, 90, 92 responses to Morant Bay Riot, x, 8-9, 108-116 passim correspondence, xvi, x, 4, 29; views on native missionaries, xi, 8, 19, 41, 58, 62; emotive preaching, xi, 76, 80; deplore lack of spirituality, xvii, 28, 30, 38, 48; heyday of, 2, 10-13 passim; declines in influence, 3, 28, 29-44 passim, 84; financial problems, 4, 27, 29, 32, 36-7, 84; alarmed by native Baptists, 7, 10, 69, 78, 82, 107; missionary cultured, 8, 32, 35, 46, 67, 84; wives and families, 13, 34, 37, 41, 66, 67, 82; seen as whites, 11, 41, 80, 82, 108; promotion of free villages, 26-29 passim; approach to Underhill meetings, 104. *See also* BMS, CMS, LMS, MMS, WMMS

Ex-slaves: prepared for freedom, ix, 1; secular interest in Christianity, xvii; defining identity, 2, 9, 84; desire for literacy 5,

Index

13, 14; grateful for missionary support, 12, 27, 85; free villages, 26-29 passim; sustaining missions, 32, 85; decreasingly an agricultural workforce, 120. *See also* Free villages and settlements

Ex-leaders: defecting to native Christian groups, 5, 28, 31, 33, 72, 73, 74, 77; forming independent groups, 5, 33, 77

Fasts: 76, 81, 106

Fletcher, Duncan (LMS): examiner, 22, 23-24, biographer of G. W. Gordon, 129 fn24; on Great Revival, 89-90, 92; social principles of, 104

Foote, Alexander (Jamaican WMMS): coloured pastor, 52, 66; in Manchioneal, 61; on strong need for Jamaican ministry, 61-62; challenging WMMS, 65, 66; on Great Revival, 87, 91; in Morant Bay aftermath, 113; transfers to Established Church

Free Blacks and Coloureds mission chapels as arena for, viii, x, xiii, xiv, 11; models for aspiring ex-slaves, ix, 11; freeholders, 11

Formal/ mainstream churches (after 1870): Jamaica Council of Churches xi, 126; majority European clergy, 121; native ministry progressing, 121, 126; role of in secondary education, 121; denominational competition, 122; status of members, 122; Jamaicanisation experiments, 123; criticism of "Colonial Christianity", 124

Free villages: land purchase for, 2; missionary input for, 2, 26-29, passim, 45, 131 fn3; independent, 28-29, 46; losing socioeconomic status, 2

Freedom: varied ideas at emancipation, ix, xv, xvi; promoted by black preachers, xv; for variety of worship, 2, 70; for US landed slaves, 6, 97, 98; to choose employer, 27; problems of, 70. *See also* Employment and poverty

Freeholders: eligible to vote, 12; rapid expansion of 12, 26, 28; supporting native Baptists, 81. *See also* Free villages

Funerals (burials): Euro-Christians, xiv, 27, 34, 37, 40; Afro-Christian, xiv, 79-80, 94

Gardner, William (LMS): Mutual improvement societies, 22-23; author of History of Jamaica, 129 fn27, views on Underhill; Letter, 103-104; afterthoughts on Morant Bay Riot, 110-111

Garvey, Marcus: xi, 121, 125

Geddes, Thomas (Jamaican WMMS): letters to WMMS, 52, 65; on the Great Revival, 92, 124

Gordon, George William: manifesto of , 1; at Underhill meetings, 100, 118; religious views of, 103-104, 106-107; taken to Morant Bay, 109, 118; hanged, 111

Governors: Eyre, alarmed by native Baptists, 74, 104; distributes Underhill Letter, 100; actions after Morant Bay Riot, 109; fears islandwide revolt, 110; criticised, 111, 115, 117, 118; John Peter Grant, 114

Great Revivial: popular movement, 6-7, 94; demonstrative penitence during, 85, 86, 89; discussed, 86-95 passim

Haiti: xv, 97

Harrison, Robert (US Consul): deplores black American landings in Jamaica, 5-6, 97; warns against missionaries travelling to US, 97, 98

Hearers/attenders: slave and free, viii; uncommitted, xiii; large number at services, 10, 29

Hillyer, William (LMS): examiner, 21; schoolmaster, 54, 55, 56; ordained, 57; on Great Revival, 91

Holland, Edward (LMS): centre of Mount Zion dispute, 54, 55, 56

House of Assembly: heavy taxation by, 7; first coloured members in, 11, 66; failure to get freeholder representation to, 12; immigration schemes of, 36; compensation for destroyed chapels, 33, 36, 128 fn3; reactions to Morant Bay Riot, 118

Illiteracy: related to spirit-led religion, 3, 74; of black preachers and leaders, 4, 74-75; prevailing, 107

Indentured labour/immigrant workers: reduced Jamaican wages and employment, 3, 31; Indian, 50; African, 83-84, 91

Independence of Jamaica: 122, 126

Independent Christian groups: community based, x, 1, 3, 8; little recognition in courts of law, xi; mutual solidarity, xi, xvi, 70, 74, 84; rapid growth of 23, 33, 97; localised/accessible, 3, 74, 97, 120;

147

no coordination between, 69, 97; rival missions, 71, 82; Myal survivals in, 82-83, 92; articulating social protest, 105, 120

Independent Methodists/ Pennockites: participation in worship, 2, 4; breakaway from WMMS, 34, 71-72; stations, 40, 71; ignored by missions, 71

Jamaica Baptist Union: request Underhill visit, 100, 118; analyse current social distress, 101-102, 105; JBU pastors, E. Hewett, 104; E. Palmer, 104; D. East, 118. *See also* Baptist Missionary Society.

Jamaican missionary/pastors: as social commentators, xvi, 7, 43, 52; empathy with own people, 50, 60, 66, 124; needed to replace European missionaries, 59; varied missionary responses to xvi, 8, 19, 41, 59, 60, 62; some adopting European social conventions, 61; outdoor preaching and home visits, 61; sustained commitment to conversion, 62; jealous of reputation, 66; in St. Thomas-in-the-East, 105; reactions to Morant Bay Riot, 112-118 passim

Jamaica Royal Commission (JRC) 1866: Beckwith's evidence, 2, 69; disconcerted by native Baptists, 69, 70, 119; 730 "witnesses", 119

Jesus Christ: not known, 40; inferior to John the Baptist, 76, 78; the saviour, 78; crucifixion of, 78, 79; no need for after baptism, 79; the merciful, 80; cited by Myal group, 83; impersonated in Great Revival, 91; visions of, 92

John the Baptist, precedence over Jesus Christ: 74, 76, 78

Johnson, Robert: (Jamaican WMMS): in St Ann, 37, 61; same salary as European missionaries, 64; resignation, 67; ordained, 132 fn44; warns of native Baptist in Vere, 72

Jordon, Edward: 34

Kellick, Parson: 71, 81

Kingston: native Baptist chapels in, 4, 7, 71, 81, 106, 107, 110; chapels in, 34, 48, 71; juvenile crime in, 43; BMS chapel in, 77; LMS chapel in, 77; release of American slaves in, 98

Knibb, William (BMS): support of ex-slaves, 12; political parson, 12; need for native ministry, 19; reports on freeholders, 26, 27; advice on raising loans, 33; criticises Established Church, 39; saving American slaves, 97-98

Kumina, 83-84, 123

Labour force: xvii, 2, 3, 11, 12, 13, 27

Land: unobtainable, ix; petitioned for, 8, 101; aspect of social mobility, 12-13; aspiration for, 26; acquisition of, 28, 45; Underhill proposal on, 101; for rent, 103

Language: rhetorical, xiv, xvii; biblical, xvii, 100, 122; of the schools, 8, 105, 118; unschooled, 8, 105

Leaders/deacons/aids: bedrock of missions, viii, xiii, 33, 45, 77; outnumbering missionaries, xiv; maintaining religious observance, xiv, 33; monitoring morality, xiv, 33, 76, 77; of native groups, xv, 3, 4, 33, 34, 70, 71, 72, 73, 80, 81, 124; defecting to native groups, 5, 28, 31, 33, 72, 73, 74, 77; emigrating, 35

Liele, George (American black Baptist): 4, 71

Lindo, Alexander (Jamaican LMS): critical of Established Church, 39; supporting Morant Bay members in keeping chapel, 44; as teaching/catechist, 57; first Jamaican LMS missionary, 58, 59; protesting drive in Porus, 61; protesting salary differentials, 63; condemns Morant Bay Riot, 112-113

Literacy: access to Bible and Christian literature, x, xvii; growing ability to communicate, xi, xvi, 59; access to wider reading, xvii, 75; thirst for, 5, 13, 14, 16; applied to protest, 74; early native Baptist disregard for, 74, 75; sought by African immigrants, 84

Loans/debts: 46, 47, 48, 49

London Missionary Society (LMS): Ridgemount Academy, 21-22; Jamaican assistant missionaries, 22, 59; free village, 28; too exacting to attract candidates, 38, 77; nondenominational, 40, 72; members accepting upkeep of missionaries, 49-50; Mount Zion dispute, 54-56; preference for ordained minister over schoolmaster, 54, ordaining schoolmasters, 57; removing missionaries, 58-59; seeking different stations from

Index

earlier missions, 71; contentions with native Baptists, 72-73, 77, 80; growing preference for Jamaican pastors, 81; chapels invaded in Great Revival, 89; views on Great Revival, 92; views on Underhill Letter, 103-104; in St Thomas-in-the-East, 105

LMS missionaries: G. Wheeler, 37; J. Gibson, J. Milne, P. Lillie, 57; B. Franklin, 57-58; J. Andrew, 58-59; W. Barrett, 73; W. Alloway, 89-108, G. Wilkinson, 81; T. Clark, 23, 109; W. Harty, 113-114. *See also* D. Fletcher, W. Gardner, A. Lindo, Woolridge

Lord's Supper/drawing to table: missionary, 5, 81; independent religious groups', 92, 103

Magistrates: planter dominated, 8; harsh on ex-slaves, 11, 99, 102-103; alarmed by native Baptist, 69; freeing landed American slaves, 96, 97, 99

Maroons after Morant Bay Riot: 107, 113, 114-115

Marriage: for mission membership, 27, 121; in Great Revival, 87, 90, 91; common law

Martrial law: 9, 70, 107, 113, 114-115

McLean, Barrett (LMS teacher/ catechist): 20-21, 129 fn26

Mearns, John (Chairman WMMS): response to Morant Bay Riot, 111-112; as chairman, 116-117

Medical services: missionary contribution to, 3, 30, 37; dearth of colonial medical officers, 3, 37, 101

Membership of missions: fluctuating, viii, 10, 27, 37-8, 12; advantage of, xvii, 8, 11, 96, 112, 113, 122; chapel responsibilities, xv, 2, 28, 9; expressing opinions, xvi, 7, 18, 41, 52-54; a nonconformist voice, xvi; attracted by literacy classes an schools, 13, 14, 15; building chapels and mission premises, 7, 27, 33; failure of day schools to attract, 17, 42; upkeep of missionaries, 27-28, 49; requiring resident ministers and teachers, 29, 31; financial involvement of 32, 35, 36, 49, 59, 64; discussed as Jamaican initiative, 45-68 passim; transference of allegiance, xiv, 2, 7, 28, 31, 39, 45, 59, 64, 67, 70, 72, 73, 77, 82, 96-97; in Great Revival, 87, 90, 93. *See also* individual missions

Mico Institution: 15, 128 fn13, 32-33, 39, 40, 53

Migration: inland, 25, 32, 40, 48, 74; overseas, 35, 40, 48, 53, 104, 122

Montego Bay: BMS chapel in, 30; epidemics in, 30; native Baptists in, 38; in Great Revival, 90-91

Morant Bay: evening classes in, 16; Jamaican pastors in, 52; native Baptist in, 49, 75, 81, 94; 105-106, 107; Underhill meeting, 104; unhealthy for European missionaries, 105

Morant Bay Riot: reactions to, 8; suppression of, 16, 139; feared as islandwide, 16; incidents in, 107, 124, 151-152; mentioned 93, 99, 104; Bogle on the run, 177. *See also* European missionaries, responses to

Moravian mission (MMS): arrival in central and western parishes viii, 29, 128 fn2; free villages regretted, 28, 43-44; Effects of schools, 17, 29, 30; Fairfield Training School, 19, 31, 39, 51, 78; Jamaican missionaries to W. Africa, 30; aids, 70. *See also* J. Buchner, A. Monteith

Murray, W. Clark (Jamaican WMMS): allegiance to, 52; addresses WMMS on status, 66; Notes growth on native Baptists, 94; in Bath after Morant Bay Riot, 114-117 passim

Myal: adoption of Christian symbols, xiv; infiltration into native Baptist groups, 2, 14, 51, 82-83, 84, 92, 110, 124; practices to deal with evils, 7, 37; medicine, 38, 56, 74, 82, 121; revival, 1842, 82-83, 121, 122, 137, 139; in Great Revival, 14, 86, 88, 92, 93, 135; spirit worship, 84; absorbed into Revival cults, 94-95, 123

Native Baptists: meeting houses, xi, xv, 5, 72, 75, 81, 107; uncoordinated groups, ix, 71, 110; daddies/leaders, ix, 2, 106, 118; blamed for Morant Bay Riot, ix, 8; community solidarity, x, xi, xv, 3, 9, 10, 13, 33; black awareness; x, xi, 80, 99; prayer meetings, xiii, xv; black preachers, xv, 4, 33, 34, 71, 72, 73, 78, 80, 81, 124; Myalism among, 2, 110; participation in worship, 2, 73, 76, 120;

Index

no early schools, 4, 55, 75, 81; opposing missionary rivalry, 4, 69, 71, 72-73; call themselves Baptists, 4, 70; expansion of, 33, 77, 94, 96; in remote settlements, 46, 55-56, 67, 71, 80, 106, 176; copying mission practices, 72, 107, 108, 109; no islandwide organisation, 73, 94; bowing down, 76; in Great Revival, 92, 93, 94. *See also* Independent Religious groups, P. Bogle, G.W. Gordon

Native ministry: *See* Jamaican missionaries/pastors

Natural disasters: 1, 3, 7, 8, 11, 48, 52

Nuttall, Enos: 24, 117

Obeah: men, 76, 113; African-born 23, 83, 134-135; activities in Great Revival, 91

Osborn, Robert: 1, 51, 34

Parishes: Western, 4, 7, 26; St Thomas-in-the-East, 4, 8, 83, 91, 94, 99, 105-107, 111-119, 124; St Catherine, 4, 26, 38; Clarendon, 4, 28, 47, 50, 72; Central parishes, 17; Trelawny, 26, 27, 62, 108; St Ann, 26, 61, 72, 100, 107, 108; St James, 26, 73, 111; St Thomas- in-the-Vale, 26, 42; St Mary, 26; Manchester, 26, 61, 62, 72; Hanover, 26, 104; Vere, 37; St Andrew, 48; Westmoreland, 61, 83, 86; St Elizabeth, 62; St David, 70; Eastern parishes, 86, 87; Portland, 115

Participation: in Chapel responsibilities, viii, xiv, xv, xvi, 27, 127; in chapel services, xiv, 81; in native group worship, 2, 73, 74, 76, 84, 120; in native group decision making, 5, 80, 85, 96, 107, 120

Pennock, Thomas (Chairman WMMS): 34, 51

Penneck, Daddy, 75

Pentecostalism: 95, 123

Petitions: belief in, xvi-xvii; from chapel members, 5, 6, 28, 33-34, 52-54, 54-56, 57-58; from small farmers, 15-16, 38; facilitated by literacy, 74; of the Poor People of St Ann, 104-105, 107; of the people of St Thomas-in-the-East, 101, 104-105; of missionaries for the Jamaica Royal Commission, 111

Phillippo, James: thinks conversion nearly achieved, 10; in the Spanish Town chapel dispute, 34, 53-54; schools started, 14; free villages started, 26, 27;
inroads on Porus, 40

Plantocracy: fear of emancipation, xv; decline in hostility to missionaries, 11; exploitation of ex-slaves, 11, 26; use of chile labour, 15; selling up land, 28; missionary sympathy for Sugar Duties Act, 41; seen as oppressors, 99

Pocomania: 84, 95, 120, 123

Police/constables: 2, 108, 125

Poverty: growing, viii, 42; persistent, xvi, 3, 7, 70, 93; subsistance living, 3, 32, 101; destitution, 36, 73; in remote settlements, 46, 47, 107; effects of, 101-102; alleviation of, 104; as a religious concern, 121

Preachers: pioneer, viii; Black American Baptist, xiii, 6, 75; missionary, xiii, 15, 30, 31, 32, 36 80, 121; native Baptist, xiv, xv, 33, 34, 71, 72, 73, 74, 80, 81, 124; travelling, xv, 4, 72; black independent, 4, 5, 15, 80, 88, 124; Pentecostal, 123

Prebyterians: 30-31, 38, 41, 128 fn2; Montego Bay Training School, 18, 19

Prices in American Civil War: 7, 93

Queen of England: loyalty to, 100, 105, 108, 109, 111; appealed to, 101, 105

Rastafarians: xi, 121, 125

Repentance: missionary emphasis, xi, 7, 31, 76, 79, 80, 114; fervent in Great Revival, 7, 14, 85, 87, 88, 89, 129

Respectability: as defined by missionary values, ix, xvi, 8, 36, 44, 46, 64; based on European moral values, 85, 120; a choice of life style, 4, 46, 71, 107; achieved by minority, 96, 104, 112, 146; decline of, 101-102, 144-145

Revivalists: 84, 95, 120, 123, 124

Roman Catholics: 40, 67, 96, 123

Savage, John: 18, 19, 30-31

Schooling, day/elementary: three Rs, xvii, 9, 74; helping leavers to avoid land work, 2, 5, 12, 14, 16; afforded by minority, 2, 3, 17, 25, 27; useful knowledge rote learnt, 5, 14, 74, 76, 80; nursery for teachers and leaders, 14, 16; popular for secular results, 15, 16, 17

Settlements: maintaining black preachers, 4, 5; effects of dispersal of, 12, 16, 29, 42,

Index

43, 46, 62; trying to emulate missionary free villages, 28-29, 40; native Baptists in, 45, 55-56, 69, 71, 80, 81
Sharpe, Sam: 11
Sins: Missionary personal, 7, 31, 39, 76, 87, 90, 107; Jamaican interpersonal, 76; repented at Great Revival, 89
Slaves: attraction of Christianity for viii, xiv-xv; having savings from sales and services, ix; American freed in Jamaica, 6, 97-98
Small holders/farmers: food crops for markets, 32; pimento and banana export, 32, 122; as successful "yeomanry", 42, 96; proposed diversity of crops, 122
Social consciences: xvi, 8, 67, 96-119 passim
Social mobility: achieved by a minority, ix, 1, 85, 122; through schooling, 5, 14, 18, 25; through chapel membership, 8, 12, 113, 122. *See also* Status
Spanish Town: Phillippo's schools in, 14; BMS chapel dispute in, 33-34, 52-54, epidemic in, 37-38; Jamaican missionaries to W. Africa from, 51; independent Baptist chapel in, 54, 71; native Baptists in, 71; resolutions of Underhill meeting at, 104
Spirits: worship of, 74, 75, 76; laying of evil, 7, 80, 82-83, 94; possession by, 3, 76, 84, 92, 94, of departed, 94; guidance of, 99, 124
Sugar Duties Act, missionaries memorial against: 36, 41-42
Sugar production: decline in 1, 2, 27, 31, 41-42, 104; closing down, 3; rivalry of slave worked, 41; failure of, 42
Sunday schools: 2, 4, 8, 13, 74
Status: anticipated in freedom, ix; in chapel membership, xv, 2, 28; in chapel responsibilities, xv, 45, 50; in independent religious groups, xv, 96; in "respectable" lifestyle, 2; in occupations open to school leavers, 2, 14, 15, 16, 17; in new freedom, 10; for middle class ranking, 25; for freeholders, 28, 46; of Jamaican and European missionaries/teachers compared, 52; for coloured people, 64-65; religious allegiance related to personal, 124
Stony Gut: chapel, 5, 106, 107, 125; protest mobilised from, 70, 105; native Baptist preaching at, 106

Syncretism: African religious activity with Myal, viii, x, 3, 69, 73, 84; Myal with mission practice, xiv; Myal with native Baptist, 2, 14, 51, 82-83, 84, 92, 110, 124; Native Baptist with mission, 72, 107, 108, 109; Independents with Myal, 82-83, 92

Taxation: heavy, 7; appeals for lowering, 8, 104
Teacher/catechists: product of day schools, 2, 5, 7, 35; aspect of upward mobility, 12; kept missions alive, 19, 20, 33, 35; emerging as ministerial candidates, 59; relationship with missionaries, 61
Teachers: European, 7, 13, 20, 28, 52; Jamaican, 7, 19, 20, 52; unaffordable, 15
Training schools: denominational, 7, 19-20; limitations of as further education, 20; graduates seeking other occupations, 25
Transfers of allegiance: xiv, 2, 7, 31, 70, 82; as protest, 28, 59; to Established Church, 39; by leaders, 45, 67, 73; by Jamaican missionaries 64, 67; to native groups, 28, 31, 39, 72, 73, 74, 77, 80, 81, 96-97

Underhill Letter: attitude of missionaries to, 8, 111, 130 fn46, 102-104; JBU-informed, 99, 118; causes of distress examined, 101
Underhill meetings: manifesto for, 1; resolutions from, 8, 99-100, 104, 118; missionary views on, 104, 110, 111
United Kingdom/Britian/Mother country: mission headquarters in, x, xi; nonconformist congregations in, 9, 41, 42, 47, 109; elementary school patterns, 18; models for chapels, 27, 33; decline in resources from, 25; revival movement in, 86
United States of America: southern states of, viii, 98; pentacostalism from, xi, 95, 123; black preachers from, xiii, 6, 75, 123; Civil War in, 7, 66, 93; revival movements in, 86; government of, 97; slavery in, 97; emancipation in, 99; market, 122. *See also* R. Harrison, US Consul in Kingston

Vaz, John (Jamaican WMMS): on epidemics, 37; in Manchester, 52, 61, 62; resignation, 67; ordained, 132 fn43

151

Index

Waddell, Hope (Presbyterian): finds native Baptist leaders authoritarian, 73; active against Myal practices, 82-83

Wages: low, 3, 31-32, 36, 42; randomly paid, 3, 36; fairness sought, 12, 27; too low for payment of chapel dues, 62; people ready to work for, 103

White(s) population: provided for by Established Church, xiii; socially dominant, xv; missionaries' families seen as, 11, 41, 80, 82, 108; colonial officials, 41; thought to be target of 1865 rioters, 110

Wesleyan Methodist Mission (WMMS): no training school, 23; stations, 26, 30, 40; circuit duties, 30, 61; declining encounter with dispersed members, 33; breakaway of Pennockites, 34; members building chapels, 47; members said to prefer British pastors, 59, 64; resistance to native ministry, 59, first Jamaican missionaries, 60, 64-66; district meetings, 61, 112, 115-117; ambivalent on differential salaries, 63-64, 65; support Underhill Letter, 102-103; reputation for neutrality, 103; attitudes to native Baptists, 112, 115-117

WMMS missionaries: W. Hamm, 30; W. Stedman, 37; J. Rowden, 37; W. Holdsworth, 37, 40, 91; W. Tyson, 40, 86-87; R. Hornabrook, 43; H. Carter (Jamaican), 61, 64-65; E. Fraser (ex-slave), 64; J Corlett, 90-91; T. Raspass, 87; I. Whitehouse, 102, 108; R. Parnther (Jamaican), 113. *See also* J. Edmondson, A. Foote (Jamaican), T. Geddes (Jamaican), J. Mearns, W. Murray

Youth/young people/juveniles: in Great Revival, 6-7 migration of, 18; vagrancy, 32, 43, 102; born after emancipation, 42, 43; indifferent to chapels, 42, 102; sexual relationships of, 43; peer group encouragement, 43; criticised by missionaries, 102, 108, 112; Report of the Royal Commision on the Juvenile Population 1879, 43, 102

Zionism, 84, 95, 120

www.ingramcontent.com/pod-product-compliance
Lightning Source LLC
Chambersburg PA
CBHW051101230426
43667CB00013B/2400

*9 7 8 9 7 6 6 4 0 0 5 1 4 *